Wild I

Hand-baked sourdough artisan breads in your own kitchen

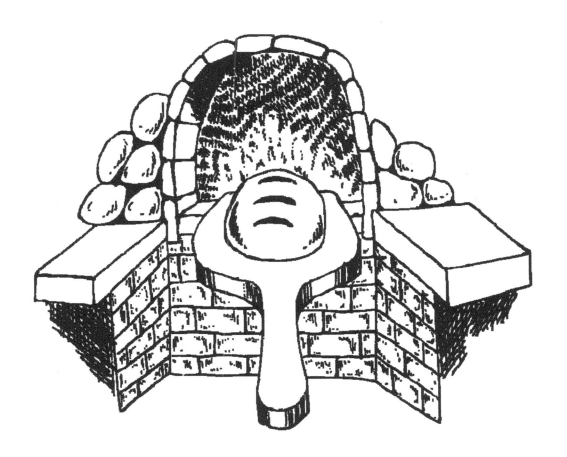

By Lisa Rayner

Wild Bread: Hand-baked sourdough artisan breads in your own kitchen

First edition, copyright © 2009 Lisa Rayner
Many of the illustrations are copyright-free historical images or clip art.
ISBN 978-0-9800608-1-2

Published and distributed by Lifeweaver LLC

P.O. Box 22324
Flagstaff, AZ 86002
Lisa@LisaRayner.com
www.LisaRayner.com

The Calendar of the Book of Hours, *16th century*.

Table of contents

Preface

Com · pan · ion: From Latin companis: com + panis, *"with-bread,"
a person who is a "sharer of bread"*

Breaking bread

By Leah Berger

Leah Berger is an expressive arts therapist and writer of high altitude poetry and prose. She enjoys baking in her earthen oven and is a lover of homemade anything, especially if it is edible. She lives in Flagstaff, Arizona. For more information about orphaned children and HIV/AIDS in Zambia please go to www.temwani.org.

I remember having tea with a group of teachers in one of the poorest areas of Lusaka, Zambia. I was there for a brief visit, as part of a volunteer trip assisting a neighborhood community severely affected by poverty and HIV/AIDS. The teachers, about 30 of them, came daily out of their own accord, to attend our workshop: "Working with Children in Grief," after having worked hard all day with large classes of children, many of them orphaned or sick, before returning home to their own families.

We always took a break to sit and have "tea." This consisted of small loaves of white bread and black tea, served British style with milk. The bread was tasteless, nutritionally deficient. Yet everybody in the room sat solemnly as one member of the group said a prayer over it, and then they all proceeded to eat it with relish. For many it was their first meal of the day.

It is from this experience that I truly learned what it means to "break bread."

I hope to never take my bread for granted, but rather to treasure the ingredients—the grain especially, for where it comes from, and the toil it took to cultivate it. I am grateful to the sun for keeping the wheat warm and feeding it, the rain for cleansing and nourishing it, the farmer who planted and threshed it, and the abundance and privilege I have in procuring it, whether that be by market or at my own hands. Most of all, I now appreciate those elements that go unseen—the bacteria and yeast that give it flavor.

This book is a great reminder to me of all of the gifts that I have right at my fingertips; that the wildness of our world can be present in the most basic and fundamental of all things. Reading about the process of making bread helps me to slow down, and my mouth waters in the anticipation of that most simple, yet palpable moment, of breaking bread. May we all be able to enjoy that moment with ease *and* nutrients someday. This book makes me think it is possible to do so.

African woman pounding grain into flour with a tall, narrow mortar and pestle.

Introduction

"There are people in the world so hungry,
that God cannot appear to them except in the form of bread."
— Mahatma Gandhi

My sourdough journey

[Neolithic era: The
"New Stone Age" that
began with the spread of
agriculture and settled
village life in the Middle
East more than 10,000
years ago]

Like many Americans, I grew up in the suburbs. I spent many an
hour playing in my neighborhood creek and a remnant patch of
woodland. From earliest childhood, I had an abiding interest in
prehistoric ways of life. As I grew up, my Neolithic instincts and
environmental sensibilities developed into an urban back-to-the-
land self-sufficiency ethic.

[Vegan: A person who
eats a 100% plant-based
diet containing no meat,
eggs, dairy or other ani-
mal-derived products]

In 1985, when I was 19, an interest in Gandhian non-violence led
me to become vegetarian, and soon after, vegan. Previously, I
had little interest in cooking. Afterwards, I began teaching
myself to cook and in the process learned that I enjoyed it.
Baking my own bread was a tantalizing dream. I tried baking
bread using commercial yeast, but the results were disappoint-
ing. The flavor just seemed—lacking somehow.

[Green revolution: the
development and spread
of industrial agriculture
worldwide beginning n
the early 1960s.]

In the last couple of decades, numerous books and articles have
been written that expose the dark side of the green revolution.
The list of horrors is long: soil erosion, deforestation, ground-
water depletion, factory farms, and the sickening effects of
industrial food on human health. Moreover, peak oil and climate
change make it imperative to find ways of growing, processing
and cooking food without the use of fossil fuels.

The bioregional food movement seeks to re-establish sustainable, local food systems. In 1993, I took a permaculture certification course. I soon decided that I wanted to get back to my Neolithic roots and learn about bioregionally-appropriate foods.

My interest in bread re-emerged. I learned that sourdough starters are the most ecologically friendly way to make bread. Unlike commercial baker's yeast, which must be bought anew for each batch of bread, sourdough cultures can live for centuries. In 1995, I began my sourdough experiments in a tiny apartment kitchen. I bought my first sourdough culture from Sourdoughs International. The Russia culture, which arrived as a dried powder, sat in my refrigerator for several weeks as I gathered up my courage to activate it. I was terrified that I would accidentally kill it! Finally, I did activate it, and I've never looked back. The Russia culture remains the source for my daily bread, although I have since experimented with other cultures.

In 1998, I traveled with my Hungarian grandmother, mother and sister to northwest Romania. My grandmother immigrated with her family from a small village outside the city of Satu Mare to Canada in 1927. My grandfather's Romanian parents immigrated from another village only seven miles away to northern New York State. My grandparents met and married in northern New York State.

We visited the village in the foothills of the Carpathian Mountains where my Romanian relatives still live as farmers, craftspeople and factory workers. One of my cousins took us to see a family home abandoned in the 1930s. The house was a classic Romanian adobe peasant house with crumbling sky-blue plaster and a broad porch on the south side. The south side windows were large, to

[Peak oil: the point in time when the maximum rate of global petroleum extraction is reached, after which the rate of production enters terminal decline]

[Bioregion: A geographical area with distinctive topography, watershed, soils, plant and animal species, and human cultures]

[Permaculture: A blend of "permanent culture" and "permanent agriculture," permaculture is a holistic design system for sustainable human environments that integrates disciplines relating to food, shelter, energy, water, plants, animals, weather, waste management and economics]

Traditional two-room peasant house from northwestern Romania.

soak up the sun's warmth, while the shady north side of the house had just two tiny 8-inch square holes for air circulation and a little extra light. The windows had no glass panes.

[Principle of multiple functions: each element in a permaculture design should perform three, or more, functions]

Inside there were two small rooms. An adobe oven was built into a bench that ran the length of the interior wall of the main room. The oven would have served multiple purposes, including baking, heating the house, counter space, sitting space, even a warm place to sleep in the winter—a perfect demonstration of the permaculture principle of multiple functions. Connecting in such a tangible way with my ancestors further piqued my interest in traditional wild breads as well as wood-fired bread ovens.

[Artisan: A skilled worker who practices some trade or handicraft]

With much practice, I gradually developed my baking skills. In 2005 I attended a free King Arthur Flour European artisan bread demonstration that provided an "aha!" moment regarding the nature of lean, wet European artisan doughs that form the core of this book. I soon began teaching sourdough artisan baking classes through my local community college.

Since 1999, I have lived in a townhome with a galley kitchen and an ordinary electric oven. I have never owned an electric mixer, bread machine or food processor, so I make my bread by hand, the old-fashioned way.

Egyptian farmers sowing emmer wheat on the flooded banks of the Nile.

Around the same time as I began my sourdough adventures, I obtained my first solar cooker. I've learned that it is possible to bake many kinds of bread in a solar cooker. I've also helped build two wood-fired earth ovens. A couple of years ago, I began grinding my own whole wheat flour by hand and growing a small plot of heirloom wheat at my neighborhood community garden.

The book

Wild Bread teaches you how to make authentic whole grain sourdough artisan breads that are easy to knead by hand and make in the variable temperatures and humidities of an ordinary kitchen.

❖ **Part I** explains the science and care of sourdough ecosystems, including how to capture your own sourdough culture from the air and where to buy authentic cultures from around the world.

❖ **Part II** explains how to make bread, including how to grind your own wholegrain flours and bake artisan-style breads in a home oven.

❖ **Part III** contains instructions for making a variety of artisan loaves, flatbreads, pan breads, batter breads, sweet rolls and more—from wheat, rye and gluten-free whole grain flours.

❖ **Part IV** introduces you to the world of sustainable bread baking, with an exploration of energy-efficient solar cookers and wood-fired earth and brick ovens.

❖ **Part V** contains a variety of information to improve your bread baking, including commercial sources for authentic sourdough culture, bread troubleshooting tips, sources for sustainably-produced grains and flours, and books and DVDs on sourdough and artisan bread baking.

Embroidered cloth decorated with wheat stalks used for wrapping Jewish Challah loaves, Israel.

My daily bread.

[Leaven: An agent added to dough or batter to make it rise and become light and porous]

[Proof: Giving yeast time to leaven a batter or dough]

How I make bread

This is a summary of the process I use to make the 100% whole wheat sourdough artisan bread described in chapter 10. As you will see, the basic process is very easy. The rest of the book provides the details.

1. Twice a week I remove a culture jar from my refrigerator the evening before baking day. I pour the culture into a bowl and feed it twice before bedtime with freshly-ground flour and water.

2. In the morning, I feed it a third time. In 1–1½ hours the starter reaches peak leavening capacity (My Russia culture is very fast. Many cultures require several hours to reach their peak).

3. Before baking, I return eight ounces of the culture to the storage jar, feed it and let it proof another 1–1½ hours and then put it back into the refrigerator.

4. I use a fork to mix the rest of the ingredients into the remaining culture, then knead the dough by hand for five minutes.

5. I let the dough rise three times, folding and shaping it in between proofs (I also make sandwich bread that requires only one proof).

6. 30–45 minutes before baking, I preheat the oven. When the bread has risen to twice its initial volume, I slash the crust and spray it with water. Then I put it in the oven and bake until done.

7. Before slicing the bread, I allow it to cool on a wire rack.

Medieval woodcut of woman carrying a basket of bread loaves.

Part 1
The nature of sourdough

"If we are what we eat, then what do we become when we eat bread from factories where human hands never touch the dough?"
— Kiko Denzer, *Build Your Own Earth Oven*

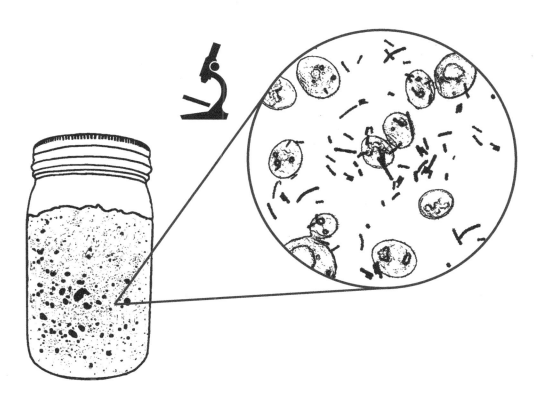

1
The history of sourdough

ش ي ع

— Aysh, Egyptian Arabic word for bread and life

The basics: Once upon a time, all bread was leavened with wild sourdough cultures. Wheat bread was the staff of life for thousands of years in the Middle East and Europe. Wild bread vanished during the heady years of the Industrial Revolution but is once again popular as people rediscover what they have lost.

[Cereal grains: Members of the Grass Family that include barley, corn, oats, rye, millet, rice, sorghum, wheat and tef]

Two ancient Egyptian words for "grain."

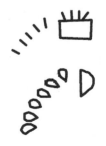

Gift of the Fertile Crescent

Wheat is a cereal grain believed to have originated in the Fertile Crescent which begins between the Tigris and Euphrates Rivers in what is today Iraq, curving north and west through Jordan, Syria and Turkey. Wild wheat species began to spread in the warmer, drier climate that arose after the end of the Ice Age. Hunter-gatherers began harvesting einkorn, the most ancient wheat species, 18,000 years ago. Einkorn's caloric contribution to the diet was a key factor in convincing early farmers to switch from a hunter-gatherer lifestyle to settled agricultural life 10,000 years ago. Other wheat species soon arose through natural hybridization, including emmer, Kamut®, durum, spelt and common wheat, also known as bread wheat.

Jared Diamond notes in his Pulitzer Prize-winning book, *Guns, Germs and Steel: The Fates of Human Societies*, that:

❖ Wheat produces high yields and has a high caloric value.
❖ Wheat kernels can be stored for long periods of time.

- ❖ Eurasia has a long east-west axis, which facilitated the diffusion of wheat cultivation across wide swaths of temperate lands with a similar climate.
- ❖ This unique set of characteristics allowed the peoples of the Middle East to develop the world's earliest cities and specialized economies based on the division of labor.

The world's first leavened breads were most likely the result of grain porridge spontaneously fermenting. Fermented porridges, breads and grain beers are found all over the world from Europe, Asia, the Middle East and Africa to North and South America. Evidence of leavened flatbread dates back 6,000 years.

The ancient Egyptians turned bread baking into an art. An ancient bakery unearthed near the Great Pyramids reveals facilities capable of baking the daily bread rations for the 30,000-plus workers who built the pyramids. In 1993, pathologist and sourdough aficionado Dr. Ed Wood traveled to Egypt with scientists from the National Geographic Society and Ancient Egypt Research Associates to attempt a recreation of ancient Egyptian sourdough bread baking. Wood captured a wild sourdough culture from the air near the pyramids and baked the breads in clay pots buried in earthen pits, as pictured on the walls of Egyptian tombs. Wood used the Egyptian wheat of choice, emmer, to make the bread.

Relief engraving of the royal bakery of Ramesses III on the walls of his tomb in the Valley of the Kings, 1151 BCE. Workers are threshing grain, kneading bread dough, shaping loaves in round, triangular and animal shapes, and baking flatbread on a large skillet.

The high regard people had for leavened bread is demonstrated in the Biblical story of Exodus; Jewish slaves fled Egypt in the middle of the night. They were in such haste that they had to leave their sourdough cultures behind. Jews abstain from leavened bread during Passover. Deuteronomy 16:3 says, "You shall eat no leavened bread with it. You shall eat unleavened bread with it seven days, even the bread of affliction; for you came forth out of the land of Egypt in haste: that you may remember the day when you came forth out of the land of Egypt all the days of your life."

The Greeks and Romans maintained public bakeries in their cities. Wood-fired earthen, brick and stone ovens were expensive to maintain, and it made more sense to run them cooperatively. During the reign of Augustus (27 BCE to14 CE) there were 329 public bakeries in Rome, a city of more than one million inhabitants. The largest of these bakeries used 1,000 bushels of spelt per day to bake 150,000 loaves of bread.

After the fall of the Roman Empire, public bakeries vanished. Like other forms of knowledge that disappeared from public view during the Dark Ages, bread baking technology survived in abbeys and monasteries. Public bakeries reappeared in 12th century Europe, again based on spelt. Affordable bread helped millions of people survive centuries of famine, war and disease. "The baker, just as much as the monk, the humanist scholar, or the architect of the great cathedrals, contributed greatly to the social progress made during the difficult period of the Middle Ages," says Ronald C. Wirtz in "Grain, Baking, and Sourdough Bread," a chapter of *Handbook of Dough Fermentations*.

European settlers to North America brought their cherished bread leavens with them. Prospectors and miners in the Far West captured their own wild sourdough cultures. Because the sourdough cultures native to the Yukon produce very sour-tasting bread, rugged Alaskan old-timers became known as "sourdoughs."

In the 1870s, scientists learned how to produce pure strains of baker's yeast, a development that allowed bread to be turned into yet another industrial product. In the 1930s active dry yeast (baker's yeast) became available to home bakers.

A carbonized loaf of spelt bread from the Roman city of Pompeii. The city was buried in volcanic ashes from Mount Vesuvius in 79 AD. This is the typical shape of a loaf from a Roman public bakery.

In the last few decades of the 20th century, naturally fermented artisan breads made a deserved comeback as people sought to regain the wonderful flavors and textures of wild bread. Renewed interest in ecological sustainability, and concerns about peak oil and climate change have created new incentives for people to learn how to maintain their own sourdough cultures. Slow food aficionados celebrate sourdough artisan breads for their rich flavors and textures, which contrast sharply with the dull, preservative-laden character of industrial bread.

Engraving of a French miller-baker from the 16th century.

[Slow food: A global movement that links the pleasure of food with a commitment to community and sustainability]

2
The ecology of sourdough

"10,000 years later, and there's no better way to raise bread!"
— Dr. Ed Wood, *World Sourdoughs From Antiquity*

The basics: Sourdough starters are referred to as "cultures." Sourdough cultures are complex ecosystems composed of multiple species of yeast and lactic acid-producing bacteria. No baker's yeast or chemical leaveners like baking soda are ever added to real sourdough breads.

[Culture: a community of microorganisms]

[Ecosystem: A community of living organisms and their physical environment linked together into a larger whole]

[Monoculture: The cultivation of a single genetically uniform organism]

[Symbiosis: A very close relationship between two or more species of living things that is necessary to their survival]

What is sourdough?

Wild sourdough yeasts don't live alone in a monoculture, like baker's yeast. Dormant cells of bacteria and fungi float through the air all around us and live in flour. When they land on a suitable material, they begin to reproduce. Their digestive process is known as "fermentation." These microorganisms live together in a mutually-beneficial symbiotic partnership like plants and animals do in larger ecosystems. The yeast and bacteria share the available nutrients rather than compete for them and cooperatively protect their ecosystem from harmful invaders.

Wild yeast

Yeast are tiny, one-celled fungi. Fungi constitute their own biological kingdom, separate from animals, plants, bacteria and protists. Sourdough yeast genera include *Saccharomyces* ("sugar-eating fungus") and *Candida*, especially *S. exiguus* (*exiguus* means "wild"). Other fungi may also be part of the ecosystem.

Sourdough yeast eat the simple sugars found in flour, including fructose and glucose. *S. exiguus* is unique because it cannot digest maltose (grain sugar composed of two linked molecules of glucose). This characteristic appears to be a coevolutionary accommodation to the lactic acid bacteria, which split apart the maltose and eat the glucose. In contrast, baker's yeast eats maltose, which puts it into competition with sourdough bacteria.

Sourdough yeast is more tolerant of varying environmental conditions such as temperature and acidity than baker's yeast. In contrast to the uniformity of baker's yeast (see "Terminator yeast" above), different strains of wild yeast produce carbon dioxide at different rates, which leads to notable differences in the leavening rates of different sourdough cultures.

When yeast have access to oxygen, aerobic fermentation produces carbon dioxide gas (CO_2), which bubbles through bread dough, making it rise. Yeast fermentation in the absence of oxygen (anaerobic fermentation) produces alcohol. A sourdough culture that has been left to ferment for a long time without being aerated will develop a thin layer of alcohol (hooch) on the surface. The alcohol provides an additional flavor dimension.

[Yeast: A collective noun that is used for both singular and plural yeast organisms]

[Genera: Related groupings of species (singular: genus). Latin names contain two parts; the first is the genus name (Saccharomyces); the second part is the species name (exiguus)]

Anaerobic fermentation is exploited to make fermented, alcoholic beverages like wine and beer.

Terminator yeast

Commercial baker's yeast is a type of brewer's (ale) yeast, *Saccharomyces cerevisae*. It is a "domesticated" yeast that has been bred for thousands of years for the rapid production of carbon dioxide gas and alcohol. It raises bread very quickly, which facilitates mass production. In contrast to the biodiversity and resiliency of sourdough cultures, baker's yeast is a genetic monoculture, similar to the hybrid corn and wheat produced on industrial farms. Baker's yeast is genetically engineered for specific leavening properties desired by industrial bakers, and produced in factories on cheap substrates such as molasses. It is bred to die after a single use, just like "terminator" seeds that prevent farmers from saving their own seeds for the next planting.

Baker's yeast long ago lost its ability to form stable symbiotic partnerships with lactic acid bacteria. In contrast to wild yeast, baker's yeast requires a low acid environment and an optimal temperature of 100°F/38°C. Stripped of their symbiotic lactobacilli, commercially baked breads have lost their flavors and natural preservatives. Artificial dough conditioners, flavors and preservatives are added to compensate for the absence of a sourdough ecosystem.

[Lactobacilli: plural; Lactobacillus: singular]

[Probiotic: Species of bacteria and yeast that are similar to beneficial microorganisms found in the human gut. Probiotic supplements are taken after the use of antibiotics to replenish the intestinal ecosystem]

One of the most famous sourdough species is L. sanfranciscensis, *which produces the unique tang of authentic San Francisco sourdough bread. Different strains of this bacteria are found all around the world.*

[pH: A scale of 1 to 14 that measures the acidity or alkalinity of a substance; 1 = very acidic, 7 = neutral, 14 = very alkaline]

Another flavorful byproduct of yeast metabolism is the amino acid glutamate. Glutamate produces a rich, savory flavor called umami (oo-MA-mee in Japanese). Umami is now known to be the fifth taste perceived by the human tongue, along with sweet, salty, sour and bitter tastes. Umami flavors are also found in other fermented foods such as miso and aged cheeses, as well as some vegetables, such as tomatoes and mushrooms.

Sourdough bacteria

Bacteria, which are single-celled organisms like yeast, are the oldest forms of life on the planet. Sourdough bacteria are lactic acid-producing bacteria (lactobacilli) that are also found in numerous other fermented foods including yogurt, kefir, sauerkraut, kimchee, lactic-fermented vegetable pickles, brined olives and traditionally brewed ginger ale and root beer.

Sourdough bacterial genera include *Lactobacillus*, *Leuconostoc* and *Streptococcus*, including probiotic species such as *Lactobacillus acidophilus*, *L. plantarum* and *L. brevis*. These bacteria produce unique flavors and textures and increase the nutritional value of sourdough bread. As we'll later see in this chapter and the next, *Leuconostoc* bacteria can sometimes cause problems in a new culture.

Sourdough bacteria eat carbohydrates, fats and proteins and produce acids, notably lactic acid and to a lesser extent acetic acid (vinegar). The pH of sourdough is roughly 4 to 4.5. Baker's yeast dough, which is lacking in lacto bacteria, has a less acidic pH of 5.5 to 6. Pathogenic microorganisms such as botulism bacteria, *E. coli* bacteria and spoilage fungi cannot reproduce in an environment with a pH below 4.6. Lactic acid bacteria produce other antibiotics to protect their ecosystems, too. Thus, the bacteria prevent pathogenic microbes from invading the sourdough ecosystem and upsetting the ecological balance. Furthermore, these natural preservatives keep sourdough bread mold-free much longer than bread made with baker's yeast.

Real sourdough flavor comes primarily from these acids. The lactobacilli need a minimum of 12 hours to ferment in order to produce these wonderful flavors. Non-sourdough breads made

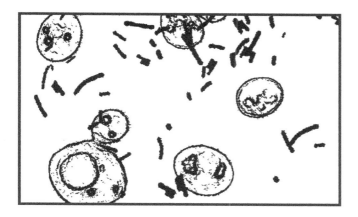

A microscopic view of a sourdough culture magnified 1000 times (not to scale). One teaspoon of healthy, active sourdough starter contains 50 million yeast cells and 5 billion lactobacilli bacteria. The much larger yeast cells reproduce by budding off smaller cells while tiny rod-shaped lactobacteria repeatedly divide themselves in half.

with baker's yeast rise so fast that there is no time for bacteria to grow, which is why modern bread lacks the flavor of wild bread. Sourdough bacteria also produce amino acids (the building blocks of protein), B vitamins, some carbon dioxide and a variety of other compounds. The amino acids create the savory aromas of crusty brown artisan breads baked at high temperatures (see chapter 7).

Ecological resilience

Just as larger ecosystems pass through stages of ecological succession as they develop, new sourdough starters likewise go through several stages. The pioneer microbes, including the sometimes troubling *Leuconostoc* bacteria, do best in the low acid environment of freshly mixed flour and water. These pioneers gradually lower the pH, making the culture increasingly acidic. Other species that need a lower pH take over and the pioneers shrink in number.

[Ecological succession: The gradual process of change in an ecosystem brought about by the replacement of one community by another in a definite order until a stable climax community is established]

In a healthy sourdough culture, lactobacilli that are good at forming symbiotic relationships with wild yeast come to dominate the culture. When the conditions are right, the yeast break their dormancy and begin to reproduce. The culture becomes light and bubbly with yeast-produced carbon dioxide and the starter develops a yeasty scent reminiscent of beer.

[Pioneer species: A species that is an early occupant of a newly created or disturbed area. A member of the earliest community in ecological succession]

Healthy sourdough ecosystems are very resilient. Once you obtain a sourdough starter culture, whether you capture it yourself from the air or buy one from a reputable source, it will remain stable even if taken to a new location. As with human

Basic sourdough definitions

Culture:	A colony of wild yeast and bacteria living in a batter of flour and water
Leaven:	A culture used to aerate bread dough with carbon dioxide gas
Mother:	A wild leaven maintained for use in baking
Pre-ferment:	A leaven made from baker's yeast designed to imitate a wild leaven
Sourdough:	The American term for a wild leaven
Sponge:	A bubbly, active sourdough culture that is ready for baking
Starter:	A jar of sourdough culture maintained for use in baking

International names for sourdough and sourdough-like pre-ferments:

Dutch:	Desem (Flemish name for starter)
Ethiopian:	Ersho (leaven for making tef injera crepes)
French:	Chef (saved piece of leavened dough)
	Levain (leaven)
	Pâte fermentée (fermented dough)
	Poolish (baker's yeast pre-ferment)
German:	Anstellgut (starter)
	Sauerteig (rye sourdough starter)
Irish:	Barm (leaven)
Italian:	Biga (sponge preferment)
	Lievito naturale (natural leaven)
	Madre acida (sourdough mother)

[Heirloom: A cultivar (variety) of a food plant or flower that was bred generations ago. The seeds are passed down through families and communities as a treasured link to the past]

families that move to a new home, change in the species composition might occur, but harmful invasion of the sourdough "household" does not happen unless the culture has been weakened in some way. However, maintaining a sourdough culture is like saving seeds from your vegetable garden for future planting. You naturally select for yeast and bacteria sub-strains that are best adapted to your conditions. In particular, strains of lacto-bacteria that are not essential to the sourdough symbiosis may disappear over time. Like heirloom seed varieties, heirloom sourdoughs can be passed down for many human generations.

Each sourdough culture contains a unique mix of yeast and bacteria strains. Wheat sourdough cultures usually contain one strain of yeast and two to four types of bacteria. The authors of *The Bread Builders* note that one "German rye-based culture contained four yeast and fourteen bacterial species, thirteen of them lactobacilli!"

Is sourdough always sour?

No! Wild bread can taste mild, sour, or anywhere in between. It's all a matter of taste. In Europe, the French use natural leavens to produce very mild artisan breads and sweet doughs, whereas the Germans and Austrians prefer strongly acidic rye breads.

Local strains of sourdough yeasts and bacteria differ from one another just as plant varieties differ from one another in different localities. Because of this natural diversity, regional sourdough breads are as distinct from one another as regional artisan cheese, miso, wine and other fermented foods and drinks. Each sourdough culture has a unique leavening time, degree of sourness and balance of additional flavors. Some strains of yeast ferment very quickly, giving less time for the bacteria to produce their acids and producing milder flavors. Other cultures, including the famous San Francisco sourdough culture, have long leavening cycles of up to 24 hours and produce very sour tasting bread. When choosing a sourdough culture, consider your family's tastes, time constraints, and other needs (this is the subject of chapter 3).

Unlike bread made with baker's yeast, most sourdough cultures ferment at room temperature. You do not need to incubate sourdoughs in special warming chambers or retard their proofing times in a refrigerator in order to create the rich flavors and textures of authentic sourdough bread. However, you can manipulate the temperature to speed up or slow down the process to better fit your schedule or produce milder or sourer breads as desired.

Mildness-sourness sourdough continuum

You'll learn about these factors and how to manipulate them throughout the book.

	More mild flavor	More sour flavor	Chapter
Bacteria:	low acid producers	high acid producers	chapter 3
Yeast:	fast yeast strain	slow yeast strain	this chapter
% of starter:	higher %	lower %	chapter 7
Flour:	high mineral (ash) content	low mineral content	chapter 5
Water content:	wetter doughs	drier doughs	chapter 7
Temperature:	warm	cool	chapter 8
Proofing time:	longer fermentation time	shorter fermentation time	chapter 8

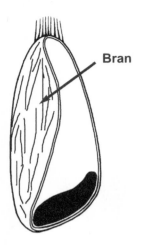

Bran

Cross section of a wheat kernel (learn more about wheat in chapter 5).

[Phytates: Phosphorus compounds that chemically bind minerals like iron and calcium, inhibiting their absorption by the body]

See the journal Applied and Environmental Microbiology, *February 2004, p. 1088-1096, Vol. 70, No. 2, "Sourdough Bread Made from Wheat and Nontoxic Flours and Started with Selected Lactobacilli Is Tolerated in Celiac Sprue Patients." Learn more about celiac disease on p. 45.*

The superior nutritional qualities of sourdough

Sourdough breads are more nutritionally complete than those made with baker's yeast. The acids produced by sourdough lactic acid bacteria and the long proofing times of sourdoughs confer a number of nutritional advantages over fast-rising breads made with baker's yeast.

Better mineral absorption

The acids produced by sourdough bacteria break down most of the anti-nutritional phytates found in the bran of cereal grains, especially wheat and rye. Whole wheat and whole rye sourdough breads contain a higher percentage of bioavailable (absorbable) minerals than non-sourdough breads and cooked whole grains. Refined wheat and rye flours do not contain bran, and therefore do not contain phytates. However, whole grain breads are much healthier than breads made with white wheat, spelt or rye flour (p. 49), so learning how to deactivate the phytates with a sourdough culture is very useful information. One study of sourdough fermentation found that the phytate content dropped by 40% after two hours of fermentation. After 48 hours only 15% of the phytates remained.

Sourdough acids also make minerals more soluble in water. Nutritionists recommend eating an acidic food with each meal to enhance mineral absorption. Sourdough bread works as well as vitamin C for this purpose.

Help for gluten sensitivities

Because gluten is a relatively new food, evolutionarily speaking, the human digestive system cannot fully digest it. The widespread appearance of gluten intolerance syndromes such as celiac disease over the last 100 years might be due to the fact that modern diets contain a lot of unmodified gluten. Lactic acid bacteria break down wheat gluten by inserting water molecules into the gluten proteins (hydrolyzation), creating forms that are less irritating to people with gluten sensitivities and allergies. Scientists are working with several strains of lactobacilli that are especially good at this process to produce wheat bread that CS sufferers can tolerate.

Lower blood sugar levels

Sourdough breads have a substantially lower glycemic index than non-sourdough breads because the lactic acid produced by sourdough bacteria slows starch digestion. A lower rank means a lower rise in blood sugar. Consistently high blood sugar levels can lead to the development of diabetes and related health problems. Breads made with white flour and baker's yeast have the same glycemic index as table sugar—100! Whole grain breads made with baker's yeast and sourdough breads made with refined hite flour have a mid-range glycemic index. One-hundred percent whole grain sourdough breads have a low glycemic index similar to whole grains and legumes.

[Glycemic index: The index (1–100) ranks foods according to how fast they raise blood sugar after a meal]

The Calendar of the Book of Hours, *16th century.*

3
Get yourself a sourdough culture

"On the frontier, a sourdough starter ... was the most important personal possession a family could have, next to the Holy Bible."
— Don and Myrtle Holm, *The Complete Sourdough Cookbook*

The basics: It's easy to obtain an authentic sourdough culture. You can:
- ❖ Capture wild yeasts and bacteria from the air
- ❖ Buy a commercial fresh or dried sourdough culture
- ❖ Get some healthy starter from a friend

Sourdough happens

Just as "compost happens" when you pile food scraps together, a batter or dough of flour and water will spontaneously ferment if left to sit in a favorable environment. All you need to provide the proper conditions for yeast and bacteria to break out of their dormancy and begin to reproduce is a simple batter of flour and water. Set out the batter for several days (indoors or outdoors), and periodically aerate it to attract the kind of species you want (aerobic or oxygen-breathing) and discourage the species you don't want (anaerobic).

The specific microbes that grow in your batter will vary depending on the region, the time of year, the weather conditions, the type of flour you use, where the bowl of batter is placed, and other factors. The best temperature for capturing a sourdough culture is room temperature, 65–75°F (18–24°C). That way, you'll be attracting strains of yeast and lacto-bacteria that will ferment well at room temperature. Avoid beginning a new starter when the temperature is above 80°F (27°C) so as not to attract bacteria species with unpleasant aromas and tastes.

You may or may not like the sourdough culture you get. Don't be discouraged if you decide that you don't like your culture. Repeat the experiment at a different time of the year or under different weather conditions if necessary.

If you wish to give starter to your friends, wait until the culture is fully active and you have decided that you like it. Then you can multiply it as desired. In fact, giving a good starter to your friends is a great way to ensure a back-up supply!

Can I make a starter with spelt, Kamut®, rye or gluten-free flour?

Yes! A sourdough culture can be made using wheat, rye or gluten-free grains.
- ❖ A wheat starter can be made with whole wheat flour, unbleached flour or ancient wheat flours like spelt and Kamut® (see chapter 5 for details on wheat flours).
- ❖ Rye starters work well for both wheat and rye breads and vice versa.
- ❖ For a gluten-free starter, use a neutral-flavored whole grain like brown rice flour. Other gluten-free flours work best for specialty breads (see below for a few examples).

Can I feed my starter different flours?

Yes. I change which type of flour I feed to my starters to activate them for baking depending on whether I am baking whole wheat, spelt, unbleached or Kamut® bread. I don't mind the fact that a residue of the previous flour will end up in my next batch of bread.

Some unusual sourdough starters
- ❖ **Flemish desem:** A desem starter is a ball of dough made of freshly ground organic whole wheat incubated inside a bag of flour at a very cool temperature for several weeks to capture wild yeasts and lactobacilli in the grain. Books that describe the desem process include *The Laurel's Kitchen Bread Book* (appendix C).
- ❖ **Ethiopian injera:** In mountainous high-altitude Ethiopia, the favored local cereal grain, tef, is used to make a sourdough crêpe called injera (p. 131).
- ❖ **South Indian idli and dosa:** These gluten-free pancakes and dumplings are made with a rice and legume sourdough starter (p. 130).
- ❖ **Greek eftazimo:** The Greeks have a special biscotti-like bread that is leavened with a sourdough starter captured in a batter made with ground garbanzo beans.

Steps to capture your own starter

1. Use a 2-quart stainless steel, glass or ceramic bowl. These materials are non-reactive. Aluminum and copper bowls are corroded by the acids produced by sourdough bacteria.

2. Because the starter is fed repeatedly for several days, it grows in volume very quickly. Begin with a small amount of batter so as not to overwhelm yourself (and your bowl collection). Whisk together 1 oz (¼ cup) flour and 2 oz (¼ cup) lukewarm, dechlorinated water. If you don't have a chlorine filter on your kitchen faucet, simmer tap water uncovered for 15 minutes and allow the water to cool to room temperature, or set out an uncovered bowl of water for 8–12 hours to allow the chlorine to evaporate.

Looking down on a bowl of bubbly sourdough batter.

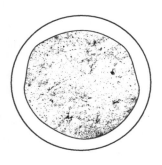

3. Set out the uncovered bowl of batter, preferably outdoors if the temperature is at least 65°F (18°C). If you are concerned about insects, cover the bowl with mesh or cheesecloth. If it is too cold or dusty outdoors, try the experiment indoors in a clean, protected location.

4. Whisk the batter vigorously at least once every 12 hours to incorporate lots of air into the batter. If the surface begins to dry out, stir the "crust" back into the batter and add more dechlorinated water or fruit juice as needed to maintain the consistency.

5. The first sourdough bubbles should appear in 2–3 days. When bubbles become visible, feed the culture with 2 tablespoons flour and enough water or acidic fruit juice (see "The pineapple juice solution," top right) to maintain the batter's consistency. Whisk vigorously to mix.

6. Continue to feed the starter every 12 hours for another 2–3 days, gradually increasing the amount of flour and water fed to the starter each time. If you have been using fruit juice, switch to water at this point). If the captured yeast are good leaveners, they will create a layer of foam 1–2 inches deep on the surface of the batter. If such foam does not appear after a total of 4–5 days since you first set out the batter, the culture may not be worth keeping. Decide whether to continue the process a little longer or start over.

The pineapple juice solution

As explained in chapter 2, *Leuconostoc* bacteria can sometimes upset the ecological balance of a new starter. In the early stages of succession, *Leuconostoc* bacteria can fool inexperienced bakers into thinking that a new starter is fully active because, unlike most lactic acid bacteria, they produce lots of carbon dioxide. They can make a new starter bubbly and light and seemingly full of active yeast, when in fact the bacteria are actually preventing the yeast from reproducing. One way to tell if your starter contains a large percentage of *Leuconostoc* bacteria is to smell it—they produce a strong musty aroma.

Bakers with King Arthur Flour, led by Debra Wink, have discovered that the process of ecological succession in a sourdough starter can be sped up, and overgrowth of *Leuconostoc* bacteria stopped in its tracks, by using pineapple juice in place of water for the first 2–3 feedings. Pineapple juice has a very low pH compared to most other fruit juices (which are also acidic, just not as acidic). By using pineapple juice in place of water, the pH of the starter remains low from the beginning of the process. A low pH prevents *Leuconostoc* bacteria from overtaking the growth of other species of lactic acid bacteria and yeast. *Leuconostoc* bacteria will still be present, but in unharmful quantities.

7. After a few days at room temperature, the batter will develop a layer of alcohol and bacteria (hooch) on the surface. This is normal. Mix the hooch back into the culture. A healthy sourdough culture has a fresh, zingy, beer-like aroma that makes your nose tingle. If the starter contains too many bacteria that don't make good sourdough citizens, the starter may develop an unpleasant smell. At this point, it can be difficult to tell whether the starter contains unwanted bacteria or is simply strong-smelling due to the long fermentation time and accumulation of organic acids and other substances produced by the bacteria. If the starter looks good visually (bubbly and not visibly contaminated by unwanted bacteria or fungi), try "washing" the starter (p. 30) before you decide on the starter's viability.

8. Once you have captured a successful sourdough culture, you may use it immediately to bake bread. **Do not forget to transfer at least 8 oz (¾ cup) of batter to a 1-quart glass jar** and feed it before refrigerating it (see the next chapter for instructions on how to maintain a sourdough culture).

Some cultures may require a few weeks or months of regular feedings at room temperature before they become a thriving, stable ecosystem. During this time, you may be overflowing with starter that can be used to bake bread, give to friends or compost.

Mail-order sources for sourdough cultures

There are only a handful of commercial sources for authentic sourdough cultures: Breadtopia.com, Friends of Carl, GEM Cultures, King Arthur Flour and Sourdoughs International. See descriptions of each culture offered by these companies in appendix A.

❖ Commercial sourdough cultures come in both fresh forms that simply need to be fed when you receive them and dried powders that must be rehydrated.

❖ Most commercial starters are maintained in refined wheat flour. However, it is easy to turn a new culture into a whole grain culture by feeding it with whole grain flours instead.

❖ Fast-rising sourdough cultures provide better "lift" when making whole grain breads. For example, Sourdoughs International sells three especially fast and vigorous cultures, the Red Sea, the Russia and the South Africa. The Red Sea and the Russia cultures have mild flavors, while the South Africa is quite sour. The South Africa is the only culture that the company has ever come across that actually leavens whole wheat doughs better than refined flour doughs.

❖ Sourdoughs International's Austria culture, which is made with wheat flour, works well for making rye bread.

❖ The only 100% rye and gluten-free sourdough cultures available commercially are sold by GEM Cultures.

Beware of fake sourdough!

Not everything described as "sourdough" is authentic.

❖ Baker's yeast cannot be used to form a functional sourdough ecosystem because it is not adapted to the acidic environment created by sourdough lactobacilli. If baker's yeast is added to a sourdough culture, the cells will die out after only a couple of generations. Never add live baker's yeast to a sourdough starter; it might upset the balance of the ecosystem.

❖ Many one-time use "sourdough" packets are mixes of baker's yeast, dried acetic acid (vinegar) and other natural and artificial flavorings. Because they contain baker's yeast and no sourdough bacteria, they are not fully functional ecosystems.

❖ Never add chemical leaveners like baking soda and baking powder to a starter. These alkaline substances will neutralize the acidic pH and kill the wild yeast and bacteria.

❖ Some books and articles erroneously state that you can obtain sourdough lactobacilli from a live yogurt culture. In actuality, the lacto bacteria found in sourdough cultures are different species and strains from those found in fermented dairy products.

Reviving a sick starter

A healthy starter can live for as long as four or more months in the refrigerator between uses—the operative word being healthy. You'll know if a starter has died because spoilage microbes will turn the jar into a Petri dish exhibiting clusters of colorful bacteria and molds. An alive but sickly starter will be very dormant when taken out of the refrigerator. Many of the yeast and bacteria will have died and it will have a thick layer of alcoholic hooch on the surface. To revive a dormant starter you'll need to feed and aerate it multiple times over a period of several days, in a process similar to the one used for activating a commercial starter. If there is a little bit of mold growth on the surface, scrape it off and pour the starter into a bowl. If the culture still seems too acidic, try "sweetening" it as described on the next page. if that doesn't work, try the "washing" procedure below the "sweetening" instructions.

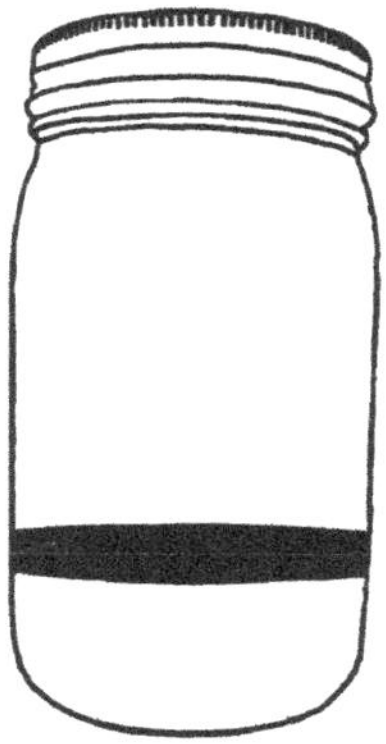

A dormant starter will have a layer of hooch on the surface.

❧ "Sweetening" a starter ☙

If the starter is runny and has an overpowering sour smell, then it is too acidic. The runniness is caused by the presence of extra alcohol, as well as acidic degradation of the gluten. If the "sweetening" process does not work to restore the culture to a healthy, bubbly condition, try "washing" as a last-ditch effort to save the culture.

1. Reserve 8 oz (¾ cup) culture and feed it with 4 oz (1 cup) flour and 4 oz (½ cup) water.
2. Proof until active (leave starter at room temperature until bubbly).
3. Return the culture to the refrigerator. Excess culture can be used to make crêpes (chapter 12) or composted.

❧ "Washing" a starter ☙

When first capturing a new culture from the air or activating a dehydrated commercial starter, the culture may become too acidic due to the overgrowth of *Leuconostoc* bacteria. In addition, a culture that has been left too long between feedings or fermented at too high a temperature may also become overly acidic or contaminated with yeast and bacterial metabolic products that inhibit growth. To restore the culture's viability, you will need to dilute it with water and feeding it to raise the pH and allow the yeast to build back up to sufficient numbers.

1. Scoop out several tablespoons of starter into a clean bowl. Compost the rest of the batter.
2. Whisk 3 cups of filtered or dechlorinated water into the culture.
3. Save one cup of diluted culture and discard the rest.
4. Whisk in another ½ cup water and 1 cup flour.
5. Proof (let the starter remain at room temperature) for about 12 hours.
6. Repeat steps 1–5 until the culture becomes more active (bubbly and foamy) and less acidic, which may take up to a week.
7. As the culture shows greater activity levels, gradually decrease the hydration level down to a spongier consistency.

❧ Drying and freezing starter ❧

Make backup starter for long-term storage. Never put fresh sourdough in the freezer. Wild yeast (*S. exiguus*) and some strains of lactic acid bacteria, including *L. sanfranciscensis*, will not survive freezing. When first dried, the microbes go dormant and the culture can then be stored in a freezer without harm.

1. Use unbleached wheat, spelt or rye flour (or white rice flour for a gluten-free starter). Whole grain oils go rancid quickly.
2. Take a few ounces of active starter. Smear a very thin layer on a piece of parchment paper or waxed paper.
3. Let it dry in a clean, undisturbed location. This will take a few days to a week depending on the humidity.
4. Peel up the starter. Crumble it and place in freezer bag or small glass jar. Store in a cool, dark location or refrigerator for up to a few months (or indefinitely in a freezer). Over time, the number of live cells will gradually decrease.
5. To reactivate, add water and flour to make a thin batter and follow the directions for activating a starter (p. 26). Feed and aerate it every 12 hours. The starter will start to bubble and foam in 1–3 days.

[Unbleached flour: Refined wheat, spelt and rye flours that have had the bran and germ removed, but that have not been subjected to artificial bleaching. Known colloquially as "white" flour. See chapter 5 for details on wheat flours and chapter 14 for information on rye flours]

Mosaic of loaves and fishes on the floor of the Church of the Multiplication of the Loaves and Fishes, Tabgha, Israel.

4
Caring for a sourdough culture

"Sin pan, no se puede comer." ("Without bread, you cannot eat.")
— Spanish proverb

The basics: Like a houseplant or a pet, a sourdough culture is alive. It needs to be fed and sheltered, rested and exercised to stay healthy. However, caring for a sourdough culture is far easier than caring for a plant or an animal. When properly cared for, a sourdough culture can live for centuries and be multiplied *ad infinitum*.

The sourdough cycle

When a jar of culture is removed from storage, it only contains a small fraction of the yeast cells needed for leavening. As a culture goes through a complete cycle of breaking dormancy—warming up, eating, breathing, reproducing and then running out of food and becoming dormant again—it fills with gas and expands in volume, then slowly loses the gas and produces a buildup of metabolitic products like alcohol, organic acids and amino acids (the building blocks of protein) that form a grayish-brown liquid layer on the top of the culture. The key idea is to feed the starter or make the dough at the peak of activity, when the yeast has the greatest leavening capacity.

Step 1: Choose a proper storage container
Step 2: Store your starter in a cool spot between uses
Step 3: Activate your starter for baking
Step 4: Save some of the culture for next time

Step 1: Choose a proper storage container

Store your starter culture in a loosely covered glass jar or ceramic crock. Never use a container made of reactive metal such as aluminum or copper; the bacterial acids will dissolve the metal. The ideal container is a one-quart wide-mouth canning jar. The tempered glass reduces the potential for shattering. The opening is wide enough to fit your hand inside for easy cleaning. Two-piece canning lids allow excess gases to escape. Don't screw the lid on tightly. Even a refrigerated starter is alive. The yeast and bacteria continue to metabolize food and produce bubbles of CO_2. If the gas cannot escape through the lid, the container may break.

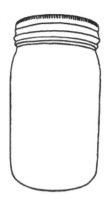

Empty one-quart wide-mouth canning jar.

The recipes in this chapter assume that you will maintain 15 oz starter. Fifteen oz fits in a one-quart canning jar, with plenty of room for expansion when the starter is active. This volume of starter can be used to bake many loaves of bread in a week. However, you can choose to maintain a greater volume of starter in a larger container if you want to open up your own sourdough bakery or something. It is also possible to store as little as 4 oz healthy starter, but baking bread would require more than three feedings to produce a usable volume of active starter for baking.

Become a naturalist

Sourdough cultures are microscopic ecosystems. While the basic process of caring for and using a sourdough culture is simple, you must get to know the individual characteristics of your culture. There are no one-size-fits-all instructions as there are for commercial baker's yeast, which is a genetically-engineered monoculture. While the basic outline of caring for a sourdough culture is common to all sourdough bakers, each baker tends to develop his or her own system over time. The directions in this chapter are designed to work with the system I use as described in this book. Once you understand the basic principles of baking with sourdough, your skills will develop to the point where you are able to modify the techniques and recipes as desired.

Observe your culture closely: How does it look, smell and taste when it is active and inactive? How much time does it take to activate and ferment at different temperatures? Keep notes on variables like temperature, humidity, length in storage, activation time, flour types, water characteristics, gluten formation in the dough, dough proofing times, etc. Use what you learn to improve your baking and as a basis for creative exploration.

Step 2: Store your starter in a cool spot

Commercial artisan bakeries use thermostatically-regulated fermentation tanks to alter the temperature and activity level of their sourdough culture as needed.

Home bakers store their sourdough starter in a refrigerator or other cool, dark place to keep the culture in suspended animation in between uses. A healthy sourdough culture can be refrigerated for several months. However, it will stay in the best shape and be easier to activate if it is used once every 1–2 weeks. The more often a starter is activated, the less dormant it becomes between uses. If used regularly, a refrigerated starter will retain visible bubbles of carbon dioxide. A culture left in the refrigerator for more than one week will enter dormancy. The leavening gases will escape, the culture will flatten and a thin layer of hooch will form on the surface. Simply stir the hooch back into the culture when you use it.

Step 3: Activate your starter for baking

[Refreshing: another term for activating a sourdough starter that has gone dormant in the refrigerator]

Activate your starter at least 8–12 hours before baking. Pour the dormant starter into a 2–6 quart glass, ceramic, plastic or stainless steel mixing bowl, depending on how much dough you will be making. If your culture is stored in a wide-mouth canning jar, a butter knife works well for scraping the culture off the sides of the jar. Wash and dry the storage container. Don't wipe the insides with a kitchen towel—you may introduce unwanted microbes.

Sourdough organisms thrive in a pure mixture of flour and water. Never add other ingredients besides flour and water to a starter because they will alter the sourdough ecosystem. Some people use bottled water, but studies show that bottled water is not necessarily more "pure" than tap water. Chlorine in tap water does have the potential to kill sourdough organisms. However, I use straight tap water and have never had a problem.

A dormant starter must be fed a minimum of three times to gradually increase its volume and allow the yeast and bacteria to increase their numbers to the point that they are numerous enough to leaven and flavor the bread. Dumping too much flour and water into a culture at one time can overwhelm the culture and give unwanted microbes a chance to multiply. Growing populations of yeast and bacteria increase exponentially (doubling and redoubling in population size multiple times). This means that you can double the amount of flour and water fed to the culture at each successive feeding. Occasionally, I cheat with only

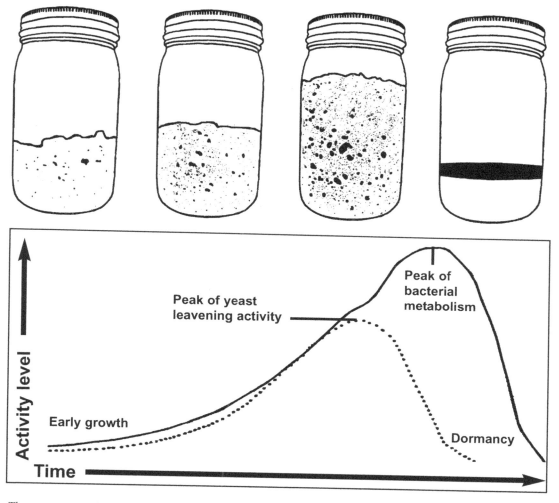

These two sets of drawings show the same sequence of sourdough culture growth and dormancy:

Row of jars (top): the first culture jar on the top left is freshly mixed starter that has been put back into the culture jar for storage. The second jar shows a few leavening bubbles created by the yeast. The third jar shows a jar of culture at its peak level of activity. The forth jar is starter that has gone dormant in a refrigerator; the culture has gone flat and a layer of alcoholic hooch has formed on top.

The graph shows that sourdough yeast (dotted curve) reach their maximum level of activity before the lactobacteria do. The bacteria continue to metabolize food and create lactic acid, amino acids and other flavorful components of sourdough for some time after the yeast have become dormant.

two feedings if I forget to take the starter out of the refrigerator early enough for three full feedings, but doing this on a regular basis can stress the culture. The time between feedings varies with the leavening speed of a sourdough culture (see below for more information about leavening speed).

Whisk the flour and water into the starter, incorporating air into the mixture. A fork or spoon works fine for small amounts of starter. A dough whisk makes it easier to mix larger volumes of dough.

Sourdough starter is flexible and can be expanded to produce exactly the amount of starter you need for baking, no more and no less. Work backwards from the amount of starter you need to figure out how many feedings and the amount of flour and water to provide at each feeding. In chapter 5, you will learn about the baker's percentage system, which allows you to scale up and calculate the amount of active starter you need.

❖ To make one loaf of bread as instructed in this book, feed your culture 2.5 oz each of flour and lukewarm water at each of the three feedings (⅝ cup flour and 5 tablespoons water). This is the minimum feeding necessary to maintain a healthy culture. Return 8 oz (¾ cup) starter to the jar for storage. There will be 22 oz starter available for baking, enough to make one to several loaves of bread. Most of my breads begin with 20 oz starter, so it's OK if a little starter sticks to the sides of the starter jar or the mixing bowl.

❖ Feeding instructions are provided in each chapter for breads requiring more or less starter.

❖ To double the active starter to 40 oz, you can add 6⅔ oz flour (1⅔ cup) and water (scant ¾ cup) at each feeding without overwhelming the microbes.

❖ To make a large volume of starter for making multiple loaves, build the starter with more than three feedings. For example, if the first feeding contained 5 oz of flour and water, the second feeding could be doubled to 10 oz and the third doubled again to 20 oz, etc. This guideline is flexible, so work backwards from the amount of starter you need to gradually expand the starter in three or more feedings.

Cover the bowl with a lid or plate. Leave the bowl at room tem-

Liquid, sponge or dough?

The consistency of a culture can vary from a pourable liquid to a "sponge" (well-aerated dough with a texture like that of a kitchen sponge) containing equal weights of flour and water (twice as much flour as water if measuring by volume) to a stiff dough. The breads in this book all begin with a sponge starter. I prefer a sponge starter because many traditional European artisan doughs begin with a sponge, even the ones that are made with a preferment (chapter 2) containing baker's yeast. Thus, it is easy to substitute an equal weight of my culture for the poolish without any modification in hydration. However, you can also convert a wetter or drier starter to a sponge consistency version by adding more flour or water as needed. (Read more about converting baker's yeast doughs to sourdoughs in chapter 5).

The differences between liquid, sponge and dough starters:

❖ The greater the water content, the more vigorous a culture will be and the easier to activate. This also means that liquid cultures run out of food faster. Therefore, liquid cultures work best when they are activated more than once a week. Conversely, drier cultures will last longer in cool storage without needing to be fed and aerated.

❖ Wetter and drier cultures have different proportions of lactobacteria. Drier cultures are more hospitable to bacteria that produce acetic acid (vinegar), the kind that produce the extra-tangy flavor of San Francisco sourdough. Wetter cultures have a greater abundance of milder-flavored lactic acid-producing bacteria.

❖ Sponges have in-between characteristics; they work well when used 3–8 times a month.

Other factors that affect the hydration level of a starter:

❖ High-acid cultures have high levels of enzymes that break down gluten protein, which creates a soupier culture consistency.

❖ Some cultures produce more alcohol than others. You can pour off the hooch before using the culture or stir it back in (extra alcolhol adds flavor you may or may not like).

❖ If you live in a dry climate, evaporation will create a drier starter, unless you add extra water to re-adjust the hydration level to your liking.

❖ The unique mix of wild yeast and bacteria in a particular starter may simply prefer more or less water to be at their most active. This is where your naturalist observation skills will come in handy.

The jar feeding method

My sourdough activation technique involves pouring all the sourdough culture in your starter jar into a bowl, feeding it three times and then returning 8 oz (¾ cup) to the jar before baking with the rest of the active culture, Obviously, if you forget to save some starter, you will lose it. Some bakers prefer to avoid such a calamity by removing only a portion of the starter jar contents for baking, and then giving the jar contents a single feeding before returning the jar to the refrigerator. I don't use this method because I have found that fully activating the entire starter with three feedings keeps my starter very active and happy. I always keep dried backup starter on hand in case I forget to return starter to the storage jar. This has only happened once in the many years I have maintained a sourdough starter.

[Proof: Giving yeast and bacteria time to ferment and leaven a batter or dough]

perature between feedings to proof. Somewhere between 65–80°F is ideal (18–27°C). At higher temperatures, the sourdough bacteria tend to multiply faster than the yeast, causing a culture to become more acidic (sour). At lower temperatures, the growth of the yeast slows considerably, greatly slowing down the leavening time. Because each culture is unique, you'll have to experiment and keep notes to learn how temperature affects the activity level of your culture. You can use the knowledge gained to alter the flavor and fermentation times to fit your baking schedule and taste preferences.

The proofing time between each feeding varies from one hour to 24 hours, depending on whether your culture is slow, intermediate or fast. Feed the culture close to its most active point, if possible. After the culture is fed, it will slowly increase its activity level up to a maximum point. At its most active, the culture will be light and spongy and may develop a top layer of foam ¼–1-inch thick. After the maximum point of activity is passed, the bubbling will slow. Eventually the sponge will collapse and liquid hooch will collect on the surface.

As the number of yeast and bacteria multiply with each feeding, the time the culture takes to become most active will decrease. Furthermore, the more often you use your starter, the faster it will reach peak leavening power. Coordinate the proofing times with your waking and sleeping schedule. For example, I remove my culture from the refrigerator about three hours before bedtime and feed it. I do the second feeding just before I go to sleep

How much starter should I use to make bread?

The amount of active sourdough starter used in a formula can vary from as little as 10% of the total weight of a dough or batter to 100%.

❖ Using a high percentage of starter results in fast rising dough. Using a low percentage of starter results in a slower rising time for the dough.

❖ My breads typically use 20 oz active starter to make one 1–1¾ lb loaf. I personally prefer the proofing periods to be fairly fast, partly because this allows my bread baking to fit into a well-defined period of time, and partly because I am impatient.

❖ You can, if you prefer, use 20 oz culture to make as many as five loaves. Simply make up the missing flour and water when you mix the dough. The initial bulk fermentation of the dough will be longer than if you use a higher percentage of culture.

❖ Highly acidic cultures work better when used as a smaller percentage of a total formula. Acid can sometimes lead to too much enzyme degradation of the flour. This can lead to a gummy bread texture (p. 64).

and the third feeding as soon as I wake up in the morning. Because I use a very fast culture, it becomes semi-dormant during its overnight feeding; the third feeding brings it back to a fully active point. I mix and knead the dough about 1½ hours after the last feeding. Most cultures require 4–8 hours to reach their peak of activity and thus need 4–8 hours between each feeding.

Fully active starter can be put in the refrigerator for up to 24 hours and taken out and used as is. It won't start to lose its "oomph" until it sits in the refrigerator for longer than 24 hours.

Step 4: Save some of the culture for next time

Before using the active culture for baking, put some of it back into the clean storage jar. If using a one-quart canning jar, return 8 oz (¾ cup) starter to the jar. If you are measuring the starter by volume (see chapter 6), stir it first to remove the carbon dioxide bubbles before you measure it. I feed my starter with 3.5 oz flour (a little less than ½ cup) and 3.5 oz water (7 tablespoons) to make a total of 15 oz of starter. All of the recipes and formulas in this book are based on this amount of starter. Again, you may wish to

Victorian illustration of two Chaldean women grinding flour between two large millstones in Babylonia.

develop your own system designed to fit your own specifications. Allow the starter in the storage jar to proof at room temperature for 1–4 hours, depending on how fast or slow the culture is, roughly until it foams up to the neck of the jar, before returning the jar to cool storage. If the starter will be stored more than a few days, return it to storage before it becomes fully active in order to save some of the available food for use during the storage period.

Part II
Peace of dough

"Makes loaves not war."
— Peace slogan

5
Wheat & flour

"Bread deals with living things, with giving life, with growth, with the seed, the grain that nurtures. It's not coincidence that we say bread is the staff of life."
— Lionel Poilâne, master French baker

The basics: The best flour for making 100% whole wheat bread is milled from hard (high protein) wheat. Whole white wheat, which has a lighter bran color than standard red wheat, is an excellent option, as is whole spelt flour. This chapter also explores the use of ancient wheats like einkorn, emmer and Kamut® in bread baking.

The many kinds of wheat

Most of the information in this chapter is about common wheat, and secondarily, spelt. The other wheat species are mentioned by name when their qualities differ from that of common wheat.

There are many species of wheat in the genus *Triticum*. Today, most bread is made with common wheat because the gluten is more elastic than that of other wheat and is thus better at holding the gas bubbles produced by yeast.

Common wheat (*Triticum x aestivum*)

Common (bread) wheat has the highest ratio of starchy endosperm to the rest of the kernel. It comes in two major varieties, "hard" wheat, which is high in gluten proteins, and "soft wheat," which is low in gluten. All-purpose flour is a mixture of the two. Hard and all-purpose flour is used for breadmaking, while soft wheat is ground into pastry flour for making tender quickbreads, cookies, cakes and pastry crusts.

The parts of a wheat kernel

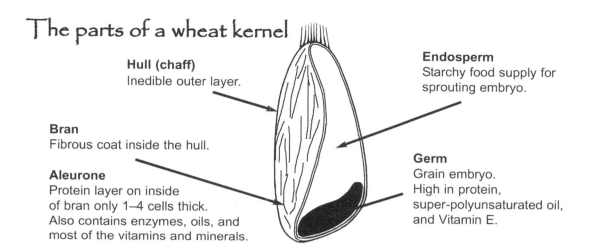

Hull (chaff)
Inedible outer layer.

Bran
Fibrous coat inside the hull.

Aleurone
Protein layer on inside
of bran only 1–4 cells thick.
Also contains enzymes, oils, and
most of the vitamins and minerals.

Endosperm
Starchy food supply for
sprouting embryo.

Germ
Grain embryo.
High in protein,
super-polyunsaturated oil,
and Vitamin E.

Durum (*T. durum*)

Durum (Latin for "hard") kernels are hard and translucent, due to their high protein content. Because of its hardness, durum was traditionally milled into coarse semolina to make pasta. Some Mediterranean breads are made with finely ground, unbleached durum flour, such as the specialty breads made in the southern Italian town of Altamura. Durum gluten is not as stretchy as that of common wheat. Durum breads require extra kneading to develop the gluten. Kneading is difficult to do by hand. Heartland Mill sells Durum Patent Flour bred specifically for bread baking (appendix C).

[Semolina: Coarsely-ground durum. Durum semolina is yellow due to the presence of carotenoids (p. 52)]

Einkorn (*T. monococcum*)

Einkorn means "one-seed" in German. Each floweret on the seedhead develops into only one seed. Einkorn has a flatter, more angular shape than common wheat and thus contains less starchy endosperm in relation to the bran and germ. It is very high in protein, but does not form a good gluten web.

Emmer (*T. dicoccon*)

Emmer was the wheat used in ancient Egyptian breadmaking. Like einkorn, emmer is high in protein, but makes poor quality gluten. Emmer berries and flour are available for sale in North America to home bakers (See Bluebird Grain Farms in appendix C).

A preserved piece of triangular-shaped Egyptian emmer bread.

Kamut (*T. durum x polonicum*)

Kamut® is a trademarked brand name based on an Ancient Egyptian word that means "soul of the Earth." The grain has a mysterious history. In 1949, a U.S. airman brought home 36 kernels to his father, a Montana wheat farmer. He was told that the grain came from the pyramids, but it was more likely a minor grain grown by farmers in Egypt and Turkey. Kamut® grains are large, light yellow in color and have a nutty flavor. Like the other ancient wheats, it is high in protein but poor in gluten. Kamut® is available to home bakers (appendix C).

Spelt (*T. spelta*)

Spelt is higher in protein than common wheat. Spelt was the major grain of the Roman Empire and was more popular in Europe than common wheat until the 1900s. European sourdough cultures coevolved with spelt flour. Spelt has a nutty flavor. It can be used on a 1:1 basis to replace common bread wheat, although breads made with 100% spelt will be a bit denser than regular wheat bread. Spelt comes in whole and refined versions (see below) and is commonly available at natural food stores and cooperatives.

Triticale (*Triticum x Secale cereale*)

Triticale (tri-ti-CALL-ee) is a wheat-rye hybrid low in gluten. Handle tricale dough like rye dough, the subject of chapter 12.

Flour quality and breadmaking

Wheat flour has a number of characteristics that affect the quality of bread. These characteristics produce breads with different textures, flavors and degree of rise.

- ❖ **Gluten quality**
- ❖ **Time of planting**
- ❖ **Level of refining (extraction rate)**
- ❖ **Length of aging/oxidation**
- ❖ **Bran color**
- ❖ **Ash (mineral) content**
- ❖ **Degree of grinding**
- ❖ **Degree of starch damage**

[Covered wheats: Einkorn, emmer and spelt. These species have outer hulls (chaff) that are firmly attached to the bran layer. Separating the wheat from the chaff was difficult before the advent of modern milling equipment. In contrast, Kamut®, durum and common wheat have easy-to-thresh hulls]

Wheat allergies and sensitivities

The types and ratios of gluten proteins found in the older wheat species cause fewer allergic reactions in people than the gluten in common bread wheat. The gliadin in these ancient grains breaks down faster during sourdough fermentation than gluten in common wheat, thus making the ancient wheats more tolerable to many wheat-sensitive people than common wheat except for the one percent of people with true wheat allergy (celiac disease). Celiac disease is diagnosed with a simple blood test that detects gluten antibodies. There are no definitive tests for non-allergy wheat sensitivities. Some research suggests that children raised on the older wheat species are less likely to develop wheat allergies and sensitivities.

However, all species of wheat contain gluten. While the ancient wheats tend to cause fewer health problems related to gluten allergy and sensitivity, they are NOT gluten-free. As mentioned in chapter 1, researchers are working on creating sourdough bread that uses special strains of lactobacilli to chemically modify wheat gluten enough to make it safe for people with celiac disease. However, none of these grains are currently suitable for people with celiac disease. This can be dangerous when commercial bakeries and natural food stores mistakenly label bread made with spelt or kamut as "wheat free."

Gluten quality

Hard high-protein flour is known as bread flour, while soft low-protein flour is known as pastry flour. Bread flour contains up to 14–18% protein. Spelt is also relatively hard. Softer wheats range from 6.5–11% protein and are used for pastries and quickbreads. All-purpose flour is a blend of hard and soft wheat.

The protein content and quality of wheat is directly related to the development of gluten—the long, flexible, rubbery strands of protein that form the structure of bread dough, creating millions of tiny air pockets that fill with the carbon dioxide gas produced by yeast. While gluten is a type of protein, not all of the proteins found in wheat link together to form gluten. Protein molecules are composed of linked chains of amino acids. Gluten is composed of two amino acids, glutenin and gliadin. When water is mixed into wheat flour, the water molecules link together with the glutenin and gliadin to create gluten.

The important thing about this information is that the ratio of glutenin to gliadin varies among different wheat species and varieties. Glutenin gives gluten its elastic strength. Gluten with a high

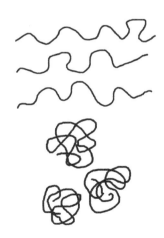

Glutenin molecules (top) are like bungee cords that link together to form a strong gluten web. Globular gliadin molecules slide past one another like ball bearings, creating extensibilty.

[The word "gluten" comes from the Latin word for glue]

How to compare the gluten contents of wheat flours:

Soft/weak wheat flour absorbs more water than hard/strong flour, thus water absorption offers a crude way to compare the protein content of flours relative to one another:

1. Measure out equal amounts of each kind of flour in separate bowls.
2. Mix an equal volume of water into each flour.
3. The higher-gluten flours will produce a firm ball of dough much more quickly than the softer ones.

proportion of glutenin is very difficult to stretch, like a tight new bungee cord. On the other hand, gliadin adds extensibility — it stretches easily. Gluten containing a higher percentage of gliadin can stretch farther without breaking, which allows it to capture bigger air bubbles, creating a lighter, fluffier texture in the finished bread. However, a very high ratio of gliadin to glutenin creates slack dough that cannot hold its shape without a pan. Gluten high in glutenin is "strong." Gluten high in gliadin is "weak."

❖ Hard common wheat and spelt have strong gluten. To make free form loaves of whole wheat European artisan bread, you must use at least 75% hard wheat or spelt flour.

❖ Durum is very high in glutenin and low in gliadin. This makes durum dough very "tight" and time-consuming to knead.

❖ The ancient wheats tend to be high in gliadin, which makes them slack and unable to hold their shape without a loaf pan.

❖ Some people like to make "flourless" Ezekiel bread from sprouted hard wheat or spelt kernels ground to a paste in a food processor and then kneaded and baked like regular dough. Sprouting activates enzymes that turn starch into malt sugar for a delicious malted flavor. However, sprouting also lowers the gluten quality. This is fine if you don't mind dense bread. You can add vital wheat gluten to such dough to increase the gluten strength. You can also dry wheat sprouts and grind them into flour, known as *panocha* (sweet flour) in Spanish.

Time of planting

Spring wheats are planted in the spring and harvested in the fall. Winter wheats are planted in the fall and harvested during spring or summer. All other things being equal, spring wheats tend to be harder than winter wheats. However, varietal and climatic differences may overwhelm this factor. It is entirely possible to grow hard winter wheat and soft spring wheat.

Level of refining (extraction rate)

If you grind up a whole wheat (or spelt) berry, you get whole wheat flour. If some or all of the bran and germ is removed, you get refined flour. Higher extraction flours contain more bran and germ than low extraction flours.

Wheat germ and bran interfere with the formation of gluten. The fat in the germ chemically weakens the gluten, resulting in softer, stickier dough. The bran physically punctures the gluten web with its sharp silicon (glass) edges. In addition, bran absorbs extra water, which also results in softer, stickier dough. In general, breads containing more bran and germ are denser and heavier than breads made with a greater percentage of refined flour. Chapters 5 and 6 explain some techniques to create fluffier, higher-rising 100% whole wheat and whole spelt breads.

Unfortunately, much of the flour labeled "whole wheat" in the United States is not 100% whole wheat. Even stone ground flour may not be 100% whole wheat. The USDA has no standards for defining whole wheat flour. Legally, retail baked goods labeled "whole wheat" need only contain 51% whole wheat flour.

Real whole wheat flour must be used within a couple of days, refrigerated up to two months or stored in a freezer for up to six months. If a package of flour has an expiration date more than six months away, be forewarned that it might not contain the germ. Sometimes wheat germ is hydrogenated just like margarine to stabilize the oil and then it is added back into the flour along with the bran.

Baking bread with ancient wheats

Ancient wheats like einkorn, emmer and Kamut® have a diverse range of flavors and textures not found in common wheat. These wheats require special handling to be used in breadmaking. Ancient wheats actually produce better-textured bread when made with sourdough cultures than when made with baker's yeast because the acids produced by sourdough bacteria chemically strengthen the gluten molecules. For example, while einkorn is very high in protein (up to 50%!), it is low in gluten proteins; what gluten it does contain is high in gliadin, so it produces a soft, extensible dough that must be proofed and baked in a loaf pan.

Ancient wheats can be added in small amounts (up to 25% of the flour) without seriously affecting the structure of the bread. Breads containing a higher percentage of ancient wheats have a dense texture but excellent flavor. If you want to use a high percentage of ancient wheats, create higher-rising, fluffier bread by adding a teaspoon of vital wheat gluten (pure gluten flour) to each cup of ancient wheat flour. Another way to incorporate ancient grains into bread is to add them in whole or cracked form. That way, they add their special flavors and nutrients without affecting the gluten structure of the dough itself.

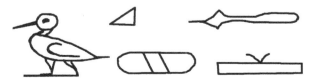

Word meaning "Large loaf" in ancient Egyptian.

Wheat flour that does not contain the germ has the same low nutritional content as white flour. If you want to make bread with real whole wheat flour, ask the manufacturer for assurance that the flour contains 100% of the germ and bran, or grind it yourself (see p. 51).

[Crumb: the interior structure of a loaf of bread; everything that isn't the crust.]

[Oxidation: The chemical reaction of a substance with oxygen]

Read about the oxidation of refined flour on p. 52.

Coin issued by Coponius, Roman governor of Judea and Samaria, 15 AD.

High speed roller milling automatically separates hulled kernels into the bran (and aleurone), germ and endosperm. The bran and germ are further ground and sifted and then mixed back into the endosperm at whatever proportion the packager desires. Wheat germ oil is highly polyunsaturated, which makes it go rancid very quickly. Furthermore, high speed roller milling heats the flour up to 400°F (204°C), above the smoke point of wheat germ oil, which further hastens its rancidity. Obviously, this is inconvenient for flour manufacturers and grocery stores, who want their products to have a long shelf life. Many millers leave out the wheat germ entirely. The resulting flour looks like it is whole wheat because of the dark flecks of bran, but most of the vitamins and minerals are missing.

Fresh versus aged flour

The gluten in freshly ground flour is very strong and elastic. It tends to shrink like a rubber band. When wheat flour is stored for several weeks, the flour naturally oxidizes. Oxygen in the air chemically reacts with the protein to relax the gluten. Dough made with freshly ground flour is less elastic than aged flour. it is more difficult to roll out and does not rise as high as oxidized flour. Because the germ in whole wheat flour goes rancid quickly, whole wheat flour cannot be aged for very long. Luckily, long slow sourdough fermentation also relaxes the gluten, offsetting the lack of oxidation. Experienced bakers disagree whether whole wheat flour should be ground fresh just before baking or first aged 2–3 weeks. I have not noticed any difference.

Bran color

Common wheat bran comes in two colors, red and white. The red color is due to a pigment that gives the flour a strong, bitter flavor. "White whole wheat" flour is quickly gaining popularity because of its lighter color and milder flavor, although white whole wheat bread still turns brown when baked. All other things being equal, red wheat has a higher gluten content than white wheat, although breeders are developing new white wheat varieties with higher protein contents. Make sure that you do not confuse white whole wheat with refined "white" flour (bleached or unbleached).

Ash (mineral) content

When grain (or another living thing) is burned, the carbon-based organic molecules evaporate. Only the ashes remain—minerals like calcium and iron. In Europe, flour is rated primarily by ash content. Higher ash content stimulates more vigorous fermentation, which creates greater dough acidity and other flavors.

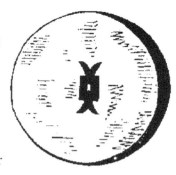

Ancient millstone.

❖ Whole grain flour contains more minerals than refined flour.

❖ Stone ground flour has a higher ash content than flour ground in a roller mill.

❖ Red wheat contains more minerals than "white" wheat.

❖ Ancient wheats contain more minerals than common wheat.

Why eat 100% whole wheat bread?

Humans today have a nearly identical genetic makeup to the first modern humans 50,000 years ago. Only 500 generations of people have been born since the beginning of the agricultural revolution 10,000 years ago. Just ten generations have lived since the start of the Industrial Revolution 250 years ago. Only two generations of people have grown up during the explosive expansion of highly refined and processed industrial foods that began midway through the 20th century. This sudden dietary shift initiated a giant societal experiment that is still revealing new health problems.

Whole wheat flour contains all of the aleurone, bran and germ in addition to the starchy endosperm. Most of the vitamins and minerals are located in the germ and aleurone layers. Refining removes these two parts along with the bran, leaving behind the endosperm. Whole wheat contains twice as many vitamins and minerals as white flour. White flour is "enriched" with a few major vitamins and minerals, but these additions in no way make up for the loss of the original nutrients, just as taking multivitamin pills does not make up for eating a poor diet.

Humans don't digest insoluble fiber, but it is important to our intestinal health. Fiber also adds to a feeling of fullness, leading one to eat less food before feeling satisfied. In addition, the fibers and oils in whole grains slow down the release of sugar into the blood stream. As explained in chapter 2, whole wheat sourdough breads have a substantially lower glycemic index than either white bread or non-sourdough breads. People who eat too many refined carbohydrates like white flour develop insulin resistance, a condition in which the high sugar loads decrease the body's ability to make insulin. Insulin resistance is the precursor to adult-onset diabetes, and increases the risks for high blood pressure, high blood levels of triglycerides, low blood levels of HDL (good cholesterol), heart disease and possibly some cancers.

Coarse, medium and finely ground flours

Flours can be ground to different degrees of fineness. Hard wheats are more difficult to grind than soft wheats, which is why durum is usually made into semolina instead of flour and why pastry flour is generally finer than high protein flours. Generally, the finer the grind, the stronger the gluten web and the lighter and fluffier the final bread. In addition, the more finely ground a flour is, the smaller the bran particles. This allows the fermentation process to break down the phytate in the bran faster, which improves the bioavailability of the minerals in the bread. However, adding a small amount of coarse flour or cracked grains to a recipe can add texture and interest.

Starch damage

Wheat starch is stored inside granules in the endosperm. Milling rips open some of the granules and exposes individual starch molecules to air and water. Hard wheat flours have the highest percentage of damaged starch.

❖ Some starch damage is necessary; exposed starch is the only kind that sourdough organisms can eat. Up to a certain point, a higher percentage of damaged starch produces a more vigorous fermentation process.

❖ Exposed starch molecules absorb more water than intact starch granules. Flour with a higher percentage of damaged starch requires more water.

❖ Flour containing lots of damaged starch produces bread with thinner, softer crust. Because European artisan breads are made with softer flours that have less damaged starch molecules than American flours, they tend to have thicker, crispier crusts.

[Atta flour: Coarsely-ground whole wheat flour used to make Indian chapati, roti, and puri breads]

[Graham flour: Whole wheat flour composed of a mix of finely-ground endosperm and coarsely-ground germ and bran. American Presbyterian minister Rev. Sylvester Graham began promoting graham flour as a health food in 1829. Today, most commercial "graham crackers" are made with refined flour colored with caramel to make them brown]

Threshing in medieval Europe.

Flour power

Lehman's Mill

I grind my own whole wheat flour with a small hand-cranked mill, Lehman's Our Best Grain Mill™, an enameled aluminum mill that consistently tests as the best hand-turned grain mill available for under $200. It has a clamp that attaches to the edge of my kitchen counter. Grain mills come in elecrtic and non-electric versions. Non-electric models with flywheels can be cranked by hand or turned into bicycle-powered versions (see *The Human Powered Home* in appendix C). High quality home-scale grain mills can be expensive. The Diamant™ cast iron mill is the one I'd really like, but it costs nearly $1,000. Sharing a grinder with friends and splitting the cost can make this quality of grinder more affordable. To find out which mill will best meet your needs, read the book *Flour Power* (appendix C).

Why I grind my own whole wheat flour

❖ It's the only inexpensive way to get real 100% stone ground flour.
❖ Hand-grinding ensures freshness.
❖ Only real whole wheat flour provides the health benefits of whole grains.
❖ I like the fact that using a hand grinder uses no electricity, and thus no fossil fuels.
❖ Hand milling provides excellent upper body exercise that balances out the lower body workouts I get from riding my bicycle and walking.

Grain mills are rated according to three features

❖ **Flour fineness:** Choose a grain mill with two round, flat synthetic "stones" or cast iron burrs. The outer stone rotates against the inner stone to grind the flour. Stone burrs are better for grinding fine wheat flour, but iron burrs are pretty good, too. The iron burrs are wonderful all-purpose burrs for grinding all kinds of grain and legume flours as well as making cracked grains and grinding nuts and seeds. I have one set of each kind. I use the stones for milling whole wheat flour and the iron burrs for milling everything else. Really cheap mills cannot grind fine wheat flour.

❖ **Grinding speed:** Some mills take a long time to grind a cup of wheat into flour, others take as little as 5 minutes. Faster mills are generally more expensive.

❖ **Cranking difficulty:** Some mills, such as the Diamant™, are designed to provide lots of leverage, which makes grinding easier. Some mills require significant muscle strength. My Lehman's mill is easy enough for an older child to use.

⅔–¾ cup wheat = 1 cup flour	10 cups wheat = 14 cups flour

[Carotenoids: Vitamin A precursors like beta-carotene]

[Potassium bromate: A common flour bleaching agent and suspected carcinogen. The chemical is banned in Canada, the European Union, and Japan. In addition, the State of California requires flour retailers to identify potassium bromate as an ingredient on the label. Flours bleached with potassium bromate are referred to as "brominated"]

Don't confuse refined white flour with whole wheat flour ground from white wheat, which has a lighter bran color than red wheat (p. 48)

Because refined flours do not contain the oily germ, they will keep for many months in a dry location. If you have a problem with grain weevils, store in a freezer or refrigerator.

Using refined flour to bake bread

While this book is mainly about baking whole grain sourdoughs, I'd like to clear up some issues about baking with refined wheat and spelt flours, also known as "white" flour.

❖ **Choose unbleached flour** for flavor and health. Refined flours are oxidized to strengthen the gluten (p. 48). Naturally-oxidized refined wheat and spelt flours are referred to as "unbleached." Unbleached flour has a cream-colored hue due to yellow-orange carotenoids in the grain. The carotenoids are the source of much of the "wheat" flavor. Some industrial millers speed up the oxidation process with artificial oxidizing agents like chlorine dioxide and potassium bromate, both suspected carcinogens. Chemical oxidation (bleaching) also destroys the carotenoids, giving bleached flour a dead white appearance. In addition, artificial oxidizing agents inhibit the growth of sourdough bacteria. Furthermore, some artificial oxidizing chemicals, including potassium bromate.

❖ **Choose hard bread flour** if you want breads with small holes and a uniform texture, such as American-style sandwich breads. Also use hard flour if you want to include some low gluten and gluten-free flours or lots of cracked grains, nuts, seeds, dried fruit, etc. The extra gluten helps to support these heavy additions ensuring proper rising.

❖ **Choose very high gluten flour** like King Arthur Flour's Sir Lancelot Hi-Gluten Flour for bagels and extra-chewy pizza crusts (appendix A).

❖ **Choose all-purpose flour** to make European-style white artisan breads. Italian Type 00 (super fine) flour is roughly similar in protein content to American all-purpose flour. Refined French bread flour (Type 55 in French terminology) contains only 11.5% protein, also similar to all-purpose flour. One difference is that French Type 55 flour contains some bran and germ. To approximate this characteristic, mix 5–10% hard whole wheat or whole spelt flour with 90–95% unbleached, all-purpose flour. Softer refined flours create the large, irregular holes characteristic of European artisan breads and are more flavorful than hard wheats due to a higher ash (mineral) content. King Arthur Flour sells a number of specialty European flours if you want exact matches (appendix A).

Baking with locally grown wheat

If you are a local food aficionado, find a local mill or agricultural cooperative that sells wheat berries or flour to retail customers. You'll have to ask the miller about the characteristics of the wheat he/she sells. The climate and soils of a particular locality have a large effect on wheat characteristics. Wheat grown in your region will be more suitable for certain types of breads than others. As we return to cooking with locally grown ingredients, bakers will develop new regional specialties that take advantage of the unique characteristics of local flours. In addition, flour ground in small batches naturally varies in protein content and ash level from batch to batch. Bakers used to uniform results must adapt to this variation.

To bake with high-quality wheat flour with rigorously defined characteristics such as gluten quality and fineness of grind, buy whole wheat berries or flour from reputable sources, such as Arrowhead Mills, Bob's Red Mill, Giusto's Vita Grain and King Arthur Flour (appendix C).

If there is no local miller, consider joining a natural foods cooperative or buying club. I belong to a small natural foods buying club in Flagstaff, Arizona that buys wholesale from United Natural Foods. Members place orders once a month. A delivery truck drops off the orders at the warehouse of a local business. I purchase 50 lb bags of hard white winter wheat. I store the grain in two 5-gallon, food-grade plastic buckets in my bedroom closet. Wheat berries stay fresh for a couple of years if stored in a dark, cool, dry location.

Growing your own wheat

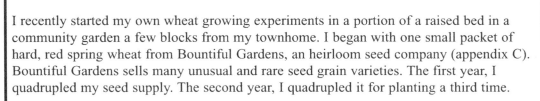

The recent decline in global wheat harvests, surging human populations and rising wheat prices have lead to a resurgence of interest in small-scale wheat growing. You don't need lots of acreage to begin your own wheat-growing journey. Even if you only have enough space to grow a handful of wheat berries, the experience will give you a much deeper appreciation for food and farmers. Wheat kernels are easily broadcast by hand in small plots. Choose easy-to-thresh common wheat, durum or Kamut®. Einkorn, emmer and spelt berries are known as "covered wheats"—they have hulls that are very difficult to remove without specialized milling equipment.

I recently started my own wheat growing experiments in a portion of a raised bed in a community garden a few blocks from my townhome. I began with one small packet of hard, red spring wheat from Bountiful Gardens, an heirloom seed company (appendix C). Bountiful Gardens sells many unusual and rare seed grain varieties. The first year, I quadrupled my seed supply. The second year, I quadrupled it for planting a third time.

6
Measuring ingredients

"All sorrows are less with bread."
— Miguel de Cervantes, *Don Quixote*

The basics: While most types of cooking offer lots of flexibility, baking good bread is a science that requires careful measuring. As you knead different types of dough, you will develop an intuitive sense of their differing qualities.

Intuition versus precision

Some people like the idea of not precisely measuring anything and instead relying on all of their senses to "organically" mix and knead their dough. You may have a grandmother or great grandmother who baked without precise measuring devices besides her hands and eyes. She may have referred to "scoops" or "handfuls" of flour and "pinches" of salt and "egg-sized" balls of butter.

I began my bread baking experiments with a purely intuitive method. Later, I learned how to weigh ingredients. I found that learning the baker's percentage system described in this chapter helped me to better understand the different types of doughs and how they create different bread textures and crusts.

Europeans traditionally buy and measure all ingredients by weight. In contrast, Americans tend to use volume measures. The problem with volume measuring is that the volume of dry ingredients, especially flour, varies according to how compacted or aerated they are. For example, one cup of wheat flour can weigh 4–6 oz, a difference that would greatly affect the consistency of a sour-dough culture or bread dough. Moreover, the moisture content of various flours, due to the atmospheric humidity level or the flours' freshness or lack thereof, also affects the weight of one cup of flour when compared to another cup of the same type of flour. In addition, salt and sugar crystal size also alters the volume.

Artisan bakers since ancient times have preferred the consistency and predictability obtained by weighing ingredients. Weighing ingredients is very precise. It's also much easier to talk about the characteristics of dough using the language of weight. Pre-weighing everything before mixing helps to avoid adding too much flour to a dough while kneading. The temptation to reduce dough stickiness by adding too much flour can lead to dry, leaden doughs. As you'll see, wetter European doughs have special characteristics not found in American-style breads. In addition, weighing ingredients will help you to develop a better intuitive feel for ingredients. This book includes weight and volume measurements for each ingredient. In order to weigh flour, you'll need a kitchen scale.

Choosing a kitchen scale

There are three types of kitchen scales: digital, spring and balance. Battery-powered digital scales are the best option for home bakers due to their precision, accuracy and affordable price of around $30 for low-end models. I use a low-priced Escali Digital Scale. Digital scales rely on electrical components, rather than a spring. Spring scales are the least accurate type of scale, which is why they are so cheap; the springs tend to wear out quickly. Balance scales used by professional bakers are very precise, however, they are not cheap; balance scales either have a pan for ingredients on one side and a platform for the weights on the other side or use a balance beam with sliding weights.

❖ If possible, choose a digital scale with increments of 0.1 oz and 1 gram. Many scales designed for home use do not measure in increments smaller than ¼ oz and 5–10 grams. For ingredients measured in smaller amounts than your scale can assess, you'll have to use volume measurements instead.

❖ Choose a digital scale with a "tare" (tear) function that allows you to place a bowl on the scale and press a button to subtract the weight of the bowl and return the balance to "0" so that you can measure ingredients in sequence directly into the bowl.

The baker's percentage system

Professional bakers do not use recipes, but "formulas" that list ingredients as ratios, rather than by specific amounts. The baker's percentage system allows bakers to easily compare different doughs at one glance and create new formulas with the desired characteristics. Furthermore, unlike recipes dependent upon volume measurements, formulas can be easily scaled up or down with no change in dough consistency. Once you understand this system, it's easy to make whatever kind of bread you want simply by knowing the percentages typical for different formulas, from dense bagels to the most delicate crêpes.

Here is the main point to remember: In the baker's percentage system, the weight of the flour is always counted as 100%. If more than one type of flour is used, the flours are added together to make 100%. The weight of all the other ingredients, such as water, fat and salt, are expressed as a percentage of the flour weight. For example, whole wheat artisan bread has a water (hydration) content of around 75%. This means that the weight of the water is equal to 75% of the weight of the flour. All the ingredients, including the flour, are then totaled to create a percentage greater than 100%. For example, if the above artisan dough has a typical 1.8% percent salt content, the total percentage (flour + water + salt) equals 176.8%. This number can then be used to scale a formula up or down to make precisely the amount of dough you desire.

Using the above artisan bread example, the formula contains 176.8 units of equal weight. Divide the weight of dough you wish to make by the number of weight units. The result is a number that is then multiplied by each ingredient percentage to calculate the required weight of each ingredient. Let's say you want to make 2 lb (32 oz) of whole wheat artisan bread:

❖ 32 oz ÷ 176.8% = 0.181
❖ 100% flour x 0.181 = 18.1 oz whole wheat flour
❖ 75% water (0.75) x 18.1 oz = 13.6 oz water
❖ 1.8% salt (0.018) x 18.1 oz = 0.3 oz salt
❖ If you begin with 20 oz sourdough starter containing 10 oz each flour and water, that leaves 8.1 oz flour and 3.6 oz water to be added to the final dough, plus the salt.

Renaissance woodcut of a miller using a windmill to grind flour.

Converting weights and measures

European formulas use the metric system. Metric is easier to use than the American system of ounces and pounds, because it is based on the decimal system (multiples of ten).

4 ounces flour (dry measure) = scant 1 cup
4 ounces water (liquid measure) = ½ cup

¼ ounce = 7 grams
1 ounce = 28 grams
1 pound = 454 grams

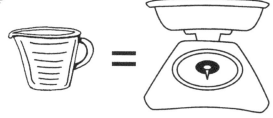

1 gram = 0.035274 ounces
10 grams = 0.35274 ounces (a little more than ⅓ oz)
1,000 grams (1 kilogram) = 35.274 ounces (2.2 lb)

The baker's percentage system makes it easy to convert non-sourdough recipes and formulas to sourdough versions. All you need to know is the weights of the ingredients. Then you substitute sourdough starter for some of the flour and water in the original recipe. Here are a few conversion tips:

❖ Many non-sourdough European artisan bread formulas begin with a preferment made with baker's yeast. The most common pre-ferment for artisan doughs is a *poolish* with a 100% hydration level (equal weights of flour and water). If your starter is maintained at a 100% hydration level, as I instruct in this book, you can directly substitute the same weight of sourdough starter in place of the preferment.

[Pre-ferment: A leaven made from baker's yeast designed to imitate sourdough]

❖ If the hydration level of your starter differs from the hydration level of a given preferment, simply add flour or water as needed to make the hydration level of the starter match the hydration level of the preferment.

❖ To convert a "straight dough" recipe to sourdough, weigh out enough active sourdough starter to equal 20–60% of the total weight of the recipe's flour and water. Then subtract the weights of the flour and water in your starter from the total weights in the recipe. Add the remaining flour and water and the rest of the ingredients and proceed as directed.

[Straight dough method: A baker's yeast method in which all dough ingredients are mixed at one time, and proofed a single time]

❖ Adapt the proofing times to accommodate the needs of your starter.

Planning your bread baking adventures

The formulas in this book are written for making a single loaf or recipe. However, it's not difficult to bake multiple loaves of one kind of bread or several different kinds of bread at one time. I frequently make at least two kinds of bread at one time, such as one freeform artisan loaf and one enriched sandwich bread or sweet dough. The key is planning ahead and calculating how much of each ingredient you'll need:

1. Decide what you want to bake: Are you making one, two or more loaves? If making multiple loaves, are you making several of one kind, or will each loaf be different?

2. Get out a sheet of paper or open up a word processor program and a calculator.

3. Begin by figuring out how much starter you will need for each loaf, and then work your way backwards to calculate:

❖ How much total starter will you need (including 8 oz to return to the starter jar)?
❖ How many feedings of the starter do you need?
❖ How large should each feeding be?
❖ Keep in mind that though sourdough is fairly flexible, don't make the initial feedings too large so as to overwhelm the sourdough ecosystem as described in the previous chapter.

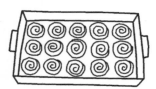

4. Write down the individual formula for each loaf. This step makes it much less likely that you'll forget to do something important during the actual dough making and baking process.

5. *Mise en place* (MEEZ-ahn-plahs) is French for "everything in place." Prior to beginning the baking process, assemble and measure each ingredient and set out each required utensil so that you won't have to remember each item as you go.

6. Measure out 8 oz active starter into the starter jar, then divide the remaining starter into individual bowls. If you are making a mix of whole wheat, unbleached and rye breads, you'll either have to compromise by making a single batch of starter containing one or more different kinds of flour, or you can choose to divide the starter into individual bowls after the first feeding, and then feed each starter a different flour for the second and third feedings.

7. To make it easier to bake each loaf in succession, if they require different baking temperatures, begin by mixing and kneading slowest rising dough (generally speaking, enriched doughs and rye breads rise more slowly than lean wheat doughs, and loaves take longer to proof than flatbread dough).

8. When it's time to bake, preheat the oven to the highest setting needed and bake the bread requiring the highest temperature first. Lower the oven temperature as needed to bake each successive type of bread.

9. Have your cooling racks in place so that you aren't scrambling when the bread is ready to come out of the oven.

Victorian woodcut of a servant girl grinding flour by hand.

7
Dough basics

"To be sensual, I think, is to respect and rejoice in the force of life, of life itself, and to be present in all that one does, from the effort of loving to the making of bread."
— James Baldwin

The basics: The most important characteristic of bread dough is its hydration level (water content). European artisan doughs are generally much wetter than American sandwich doughs. Other ingredients besides flour and water also have important effects upon dough characteristics.

The hydration level of dough

The hydration level of a dough determines the characteristics of the resulting bread crumb, the shape of freeform loaves and the thickness of the crust. Once you are familiar with the concept of dough hydration, it's easy to make or invent any kind of bread you want without a formula or recipe.

A gluten web is comprised of linked molecules of gluten proteins and water—one part protein to two parts water. The hydration level of dough can vary from as little as 40% water for very stiff bagel dough to 300% water for the thinnest crêpes. American doughs tend to be on the drier side, while European doughs tend to be wetter. Drier doughs produce a fine, even-textured crumb because their tight gluten webs inhibit rising. Wetter doughs are more extensible and thus produce the larger, more irregular holes characteristic of European breads.

Hydration percentages of dough

The lower hydration percentages for each bread type are for doughs made with unbleached flour while the higher percentages are for whole grain versions.

Dough	Hydration	Bread type
Stiff	55–58%	Bagels
Firm	58–65 %	American pan breads and sweet doughs
Moderate	65–75%	European artisan bread
Slack	75–90%	Italian ciabatta
Thick batter	90–130%	Batter (no knead) breads
Thin batter	130–150%	Pancakes
Liquid	up to 300%	Crêpes

The hydration level of a dough is also affected by the type of flour. Bran and gluten both soak up extra water. I recommend experimenting with hydration levels to get an intimate sense of how the flour to liquid ratio affects the texture of the final bread.

❖ **Whole wheat and whole rye** flours absorb more water than unbleached flour.

❖ **White whole wheat** absorbs less water than regular whole wheat, because white wheat has a thinner bran layer than red wheat.

❖ **High gluten** flours require more water than medium and low gluten flours.

❖ **European wheats**, which are lower in protein than American wheats, tend to absorb less water than hard American-grown wheats.

The major division between types of wheat bread is the one between European artisan breads and American pan breads. As mentioned above, Artisan doughs are much wetter than American bread doughs. In addition, artisan dough is "lean." It contains only flour, water and salt. Enriched American sandwich breads and sweet doughs may contain fat, sugar, milk or eggs. These additional ingredients affect gluten development and the crust and crumb characteristics of the final bread.

European artisan bread

Classic European artisan breads have a 65–67% hydration level (if made with unbleached flour) or 75% (for 100% whole wheat flour) because that is the optimum level of hydration for gluten development. Such wet, extensible doughs produce loaves with an open, irregular crumb structure. In drier doughs, there is not enough water to fully activate the gluten. In very wet doughs and batters, the gluten proteins are "swimming" in water and find it more difficult to link up with one another. Because artisan doughs have the ideal hydration level for gluten formation, they only need to be kneaded for about 3–5 minutes.

Lean doughs work well with both mild and acidic sourdough cultures. Artisan breads are baked without a pan in a freeform shape ranging from round to long and thin to flatbreads. Europeans slice artisan breads horizontally to make sandwiches. Artisan breads go stale faster than enriched breads because the crust dries out more easily and they are thus best eaten within a few days if you want a crunchy crust texture. (They keep for up to a couple of weeks when wrapped, but the crust will soften.)

Two classic European artisan breads made with lean, wet dough: A round boule (top) and flat, crusty French fougasse.

Flavor development in lean artisan bread comes from several factors:

❖ Wet dough stimulates the microbial sourdough ecosystem, leading to a greater breakdown of starches into sugars and proteins into amino acids. See "The importance of enzymes" below.

❖ Artisan breads are proofed at room temperature or cooler temperatures to allow the lactic acid bacteria to develop lots of sourdough flavor.

❖ Artisan bread is baked at high temperatures (450–600°F/232–316°C), preferably on a stone or earthen hearth. This technique is mimicked in a conventional gas or electric oven with the use of preheated baking stones or unglazed ceramic tiles. During baking the sugars and proteins produce lots of flavor and aroma and a thick, crunchy brown crust (see below and chapter 9).

A cross section of artisan bread showing its open, irregular crumb structure and thick, dark crust.

Enriched breads

The flavor in American pan breads and sweet doughs comes primarily from the additional ingredients added to the dough, although the sourdough starter itself also adds considerable flavor that is not found in pan bread made with baker's yeast. Enriched breads are baked in a pan at a moderate baking temperature to produce a thin, soft crust. The fat in enriched breads inhibits staling and thus extends the storage time for the bread.

Enriched breads contain fat, sugar and other ingredients and are baked in a pan at a moderate temperature

Enriched breads require high gluten flour and a longer kneading to fully develop the gluten and produce the fine, even crumb characteristic of sandwich breads. American pan breads, which are often sliced for sandwiches or toast, require smaller, uniform holes for proper functioning (i.e., you don't want the mustard or mayonnaise squeezing through a large hole into your hand).

True sweet doughs with a sugar content of 15–20% the weight of the flour work best with mild sourdough cultures that won't overwhelm the sweetness. Also, vigorous wild yeast strains (which tend to produce a faster rise and a milder flavor) are better at expanding dough weighed down with sugar and fat and produce a lighter, fluffier crumb.

Bread comparison

Lean European artisan breads	Enriched pan breads
Soft wet dough (high hydration %)	Stiff, dry dough (low hydration %)
Moderate protein flour	High protein flour
Lean formula	Contains fat and sugar
Short kneading	Long kneading
Cooler proofing temperature	Warmer proofing temperature
Long proofing period	Short proofing period
Freeform shape (no pan)	Proofed in a loaf pan
Baked directly on hearth	Baked in a loaf pan
High baking temperature	Moderate baking temperature
Thick, crisp dark crust	Light, thin soft crust
Open, irregular, chewy crumb	Fine, even, soft crumb
Shorter keeping qualities	Longer keeping qualities

The importance of enzymes

Enzymes are proteins that catalyze (speed up) chemical reactions in living cells. Life could not exist without them. Enzymes exist naturally in flour and are also produced by sourdough yeast and bacteria. These enzymes have a profound but under-appreciated role in breadmaking. They produce a more vigorous fermentation process and richer flavors and textures of baked bread.

In brief: Enzymes break down larger molecules into smaller ones—starches into sugars and proteins into amino acids. Why is this so important in breadmaking? Starches and proteins are bland. It's the sugars and amino acids that produce the rich flavors associated with bread, especially artisan bread. Another effect of enzyme gluten protein breakdown is to create a more extensible (easy to stretch) dough (chapter 2), which is a required characteristic for making artisan breads with a large, irregular hole structure.

When bread is baked at high temperatures, the sugars and amino acids undergo two very important flavor reactions:
  ❖ **Caramelization of sugar:** a process of controlled burn that creates richer, sweeter flavors.
  ❖ **Maillard browning:** when malt sugar reacts with amino acids (discussed in greater detail on p. 87), hundreds of new compounds form. It is these compunds that produce the quintessential aroma of baking bread. Recall the discussion in chapter 2 about how yeast metabolism produces the amino acid glutamate, which is the source for a rich, savory umami flavor. Because artisan breads are baked at a higher temperature than American loaf breads and develop a thick, dark crunchy crust they have more of that special flavor.

On the other end of the scale, runaway enzyme activity leads to dense, gummy bread because it breaks down the gluten web and starch gels that form the physical structure of dough and bread, respectively. The key is to create an optimum balance among the various forces that affect enzyme activity in bread dough. The low pH of sourdough cultures prevents runaway enzyme activity from causing problems. Here are some ways to enhance enzyme production:

Sourdough percentage

Sourdough breads have a head start on enzyme levels compared to baker's yeast doughs because active starter contains so many enzymes, as well as enzyme breakdown products like malt sugar and free amino acids. Formulas using a high percentage of active starter (like my formulas in this book) are more flavorful than those that use a small percentage of active starter to make dough. A higher percentage of starter is especially important to the presence of lactobacilli, which take at least 12 hours to produce their special flavors and acidity.

Retardation of proofing

Unlike bread made with baker's yeast, most sourdough cultures ferment at room temperature or below. When dough rises at 65°F (18°C) or below, the yeast slow down their metabolism, which greatly retards the rising process. This slowdown gives the lactobacteria considerably more time to produce enzymes, sugars and free amino acids, as well as acetic acid (vinegar). Retardation works best with mild-flavored cultures; very sour cultures will produce bread that is too sour at low temperatures.

Diastatic malt

Diastatic malt is a sweet flour produced from sprouted wheat, rye or barley. Diastatic malt is naturally high in grain enzymes (amylases) that are produced during the sprouting process. The amylases transform grain starch into malt sugar (maltose). Diastatic malt powder is available in both dry and liquid forms at natural food stores and homebrew supply stores (it's the same stuff used to brew beer). Non-diastatic malt (usually in the form of barley malt syrup) has been heated to deactivate the enzymes and is used strictly as a sweetener.

Malt sugar (maltose, $C_{12}H_{22}O_{11}$) is composed of two linked molecules of glucose, also known as blood sugar.

While amylases are found naturally in regular flour, the content varies. Commercial wheat millers enrich their wheat flours with either diastatic malt or fungal amylase (produced in a laboratory by the fungus *Aspergillus oryzae*) to ensure a proper level of enzyme functioning. However, regional or home grown wheats may or may not contain enough amylase and thus may benefit from the addition of a small amount (1 teaspoon) of diastatic malt per 1–2 lb loaf of

Make your own diastatic malt by sprouting wheat, rye or barley berries

1. Soak berries in water in a sprouting jar for 8–12 hours.
2. Drain the water, rinse and place jar upside down to drain excess moisture in a dark, warm location.
3. Repeat the rinsing and draining procedure 2–4 times per day.
4. In 2–3 days the berries will develop sprout "tails" 1/16–1/8 inch long.
5. At this point, either grind the wet sprouts in a food processor or dry them at temperatures below 130°F (54°C) (higher temperatures deactivate the enzymes) and then grind them in a home grain mill.

bread. You'll know if your wheat berries contain an adequate level of natural amylase enzymes by the vigorousness of the fermentation process, how well the dough rises and proper crust browning (dough lacking adequate amylase is sluggish and the crust is pale). Try adding some diastatic malt and see if that improves the situation (if it doesn't, a lack of amylase is probably not the source of the problems). You can also try Peter Reinhart's method for boosting amylase activity below. Beware: Too much diastatic malt will transform too much starch into sugar and create gummy dough.

Soakers

Master baker Peter Reinhart has developed a new method for boosting enzyme activity in dough. In his book *Peter Reinhart's Whole Grain Breads: New Techniques, Extraordinary Flavor*, Reinhart explains how to presoak some of a formula's flour with some of the water or milk before adding those ingredients to the active sourdough starter. This method allows the malt sugar to accumulate in greater amounts before the sourdough lactobacteria get a chance to start eating it. Thus, more malt sugar ends up in the finished bread, adding sweetness and enhancing the Maillard browning reactions during baking. Presoaked flour also softens the bran, which makes it less likely to tear the gluten web, and deactivates the phytates, which increases the bioavailability of minerals like iron and calcium (p. 22). Salt must be added to a soaker to prevent runaway enzyme activity.

In my opinion, Reinhart's method only makes sense if you choose to use a small percentage of sourdough culture in each loaf because a high percentage of sourdough culture already provides lots of pre-hydration for the flour. In addition, formulas using a high percentage of starter typically don't include enough additional water to make a soaker. Furthermore, Reinhart almost always spikes his sourdough with baker's yeast to produce a quick final proof, something I would never do. Moreover, I am not crazy about the extra-sweet malty flavor of these breads, except when making enriched breads.

If you are using the baker's percentage system, you can modify any formula to incorporate this method by making a soaker with some of the formula's flour, liquid and salt:

❖ Reinhart typically mixes a soaker containing 8 oz flour + 7 oz water, milk or yogurt + 0.14 oz (½ teaspoon) salt. I have found that wrapping a soaker in plastic wrap or a sealed storage container works well—the soaker does not stick to the wrap.

❖ Soakers can be left at room temperature for 8–24 hours or up to 3 days refrigerated (let them warm up to room temperature for 2 hours before using).

❖ To make the dough, Reinhart uses a bench knife (chapter 8) to chop the soaker and a relatively stiff active sourdough starter or baker's yeast poolish into small pieces. He then mixes the two doughs together "epoxy style," as he puts it, along with the rest of the ingredients.

❖ Because these breads contain a higher-than-normal percentage of malt sugar, they must be baked at temperatures 25–50°F lower than other breads to avoid over-caramelization (browning) of the crust.

Bench knife.

[Epoxy: epoxy-style glue made by mixing two substances together just before the glue is applied]

Mashes and scalds

Reinhart's book also discusses the Scottish Parisian Barm method revived by Monica Spiller. This method is similar to the soaker method, but the water is heated to boiling or near-boiling and stirred into some of the flour to partially pre-gelatinize the starches before baking. Gelatinization exposes the flour starches to the enzymes, and so speeds up the sugar-conversion process. Spiller notes that the process strengthens the gluten web and creates soft, light-textured whole wheat bread. Reinhart differentiates between scalds, which use boiling water, and mashes, which require water that does not go over 165°F (74°C). Reinhart prefers mashes because they are not hot enough to deactivate alpha-amylase enzymes—the ones that create malt sugar—yet hot enough to deactivate beta-amylase enzymes, too much of which will turn a dough into mush. This technique must be followed very carefully, as bad technique will lead to bread with a gummy interior.

When wheat flour is first mixed together with water, the gluten linkages (above) are haphazard. As dough is kneaded, the gluten forms chains that align into parallel strands (below).

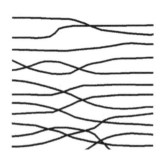

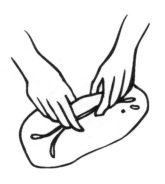

Making a good gluten web

As soon as flour and water are combined in the mixing bowl, strands of gluten begin to form. At first, the gluten is linked together haphazardly. Quickbread is baked at this stage, which is why quickbread has such a delicate, fluffy texture. Bread dough must be kneaded to break apart those random gluten linkages and realign the gluten into parallel sheets similar to muscle fibers.

The form, strength and elasticity of a gluten web are affected by several factors:

❖ **Acidity level:** Acid strengthens gluten. Sourdoughs require less mixing and kneading than doughs made with baker's yeast. On the other hand, too much acid breaks down gluten. Gluten breakdown is only a problem with starters that have been left at room temperature too long without being fed and aerated.

❖ **Hydration percentage:** As explained above, the "perfect" water percentage for whole wheat dough is about 75% and for dough made with unbleached flour, about 65%. These percentages create dough with the optimum balance of strength and elasticity. The humidity level affects how much flour must be added to the dough to achieve these percentages.

❖ **Whether dough is lean or enriched:** Lean doughs have unimpeded gluten formation, as there is nothing to get in between the gluten proteins and the water molecules. Fat and sugar interfere with gluten formation, leading to a weaker gluten web. Chapter 11 discusses these ingredients in more detail.

❖ **Type of flour:** Whole wheat and high protein unbleached flour require more mixing and kneading than other wheat flours to fully develop the gluten web. Ancient wheats require less mixing and kneading because they contain less gluten.

❖ **Salt:** Salt tightens and strengthens gluten (see right).

❖ **Mixing, kneading and shaping:** Under-processed dough contains some random gluten linkages and thus has a weaker structure that is prone to tearing and less able to hold onto the leavening gases (carbon dioxide, air and steam expansion during baking). Mixing, kneading and shaping (next chapter) oxygenate (introduce air) into the dough. Oxygen chemically relaxes gluten, producing greater dough extensibility.

❖ **Fermentation/proofing:** Proofing (next chapter) completes the development of the gluten.

Bread and salt

"Khleb da sol!" (*"Bread and salt!"*)
— Traditional Russian greeting expressing good will toward the host

Salt is added to bread for more than flavor

❖ **Salt draws water away from the yeast and bacteria,** in effect, partially dehydrating them. Salt slows down the fermentation and proofing times, allowing them to be more easily controlled. Salt concentrations above 1.8% inhibit fermentation too much.

❖ **Salt regulates enzyme activity,** preventing the runaway breakdown of starches and proteins.

❖ **Salt chemically tightens gluten,** which allows dough to be stretched farther without ripping. Dough made with primitive wheats like einkorn, which have very weak gluten, especially benefit from the addition of salt.

❖ **Salt preserves the yellow carotenoids** in whole wheat and unbleached flours that contribute to the final color and flavor.

❖ **The ideal salt concentration** in a dough is 1.8% (baker's percentage).

Types of salt

Avoid iodine-enriched salt. Iodine is toxic to sourdough microbes. Don't bother buying expensive gourmet salts — you won't notice the difference. Otherwise, any type of salt is OK for breadmaking. Large salt crystals take up twice as much volume as fine crystals. Weigh salt using the baker's percentage system for accurate measurements.

❖ **Sea salt:** The mineral residue left behind after the evaporation of sea water. "Certified organic" is solar-evaporated in nature reserves.

❖ **Mineral/table/rock salt:** Mined salt from the dried deposits of ancient seas.

❖ **Canning/pickling salt:** Pure sodium chloride crystals from any source.

❖ **Kosher salt:** Any coarse-grained or flaked salt (salt is used to cure kosher meats by absorbing blood; large salt crystals absorb more moisture than finely ground crystals).

❖ **Unrefined salt:** From any source; ranges in color from nearly clear, to white, gray, and pale shades of yellow, orange, pink, purple and brown.

8
Mixing, kneading, shaping & proofing

"Everyone is kneaded out of the same dough but not baked in the same oven."
— Yiddish proverb

The basics: Wetter European artisan doughs require more delicate kneading and degassing than American pan loaves. Simple pan loaves require just one proofing before baking while freestanding artisan loaves need several shapings and proofings to tighten the outer surface so the bread holds its shape.

Steps to making dough

The texture and shape of bread is affected by several variables:

❖ How the dough is mixed and kneaded
❖ How many times the dough is folded, degassed and reshaped during proofing
❖ The proofing temperature, number of proofs and length of each proof

Both batters and doughs must go through the following steps:
Step 1: Measuring the ingredients
Step 2: Mixing the ingredients

All doughs also require the next few steps:
Step 3: Kneading the dough
Step 4: Shaping the dough
Step 5: Bulk fermentation (first proof)
Step 6: Folding and degassing the dough

Some doughs also require the following step:
Step 7: Second proof or bench rest and rolling out

Freestanding artisan loaves require the last two steps:
Step 8: Second folding and final shaping
Step 9: Final proof

Step 1: Measuring the ingredients

Before you begin to make the dough, **don't forget to save 8 oz (¾ cup) of starter** for next time.

Weigh out the starter into the bowl (if you have fed the starter with the exact amounts of flour and water suggested in the formula, there should be exactly the right amount of starter available). If you have a kitchen scale with tare capability, leave the bowl on it and reset it to zero. Weigh out the water, salt and other non-flour ingredients such as fat, sugar, cracked grains, herbs and spices one-by-one into the bowl, resetting to zero between each addition. Some bakers don't like to add chunky ingredients like nuts or raisins at this point, because they will interfere with gluten formation.

The temperature of the water can have a large effect on the proofing times. Because sourdoughs have a longer, slower proofing period at room temperature than dough leavened with baker's yeast, it is best to use water that is also at room temperature unless you are trying to speed up or slow down the fermentation. Hot water (85°F/29°C) leads to faster proofing, and thus milder-flavored bread, because the lactobacteria don't have as much time to reproduce and produce their sourdough flavors. Cold water slows down proofing, which can be a plus if you want rich sourdough flavor (lactobacteria need at least 12 hours to fully flavor a dough).

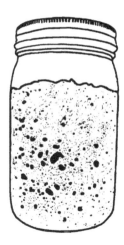

In a separate bowl, weigh out the remaining flour that will be added to the dough. This flour will be used during kneading and proofing, so you will not want to dump it into the bowl all at once.

Always remember to save some starter for next time!

Useful tools for making bread

All you really need to make bread dough are a bowl and a fork and a kneading surface. However, a few good tools make the process easier.

Baker's couche: Some artisan bread bakers fold smooth cotton, flax linen or hemp towels to create long narrow furrows for proofing long breads such as bâtards. Paper towels are another option.

Bench knife: A baker's bench knife (bencher) is a rectangular, six-inch long, stainless steel blade with an easy-to-grip handle that makes it easy to divide dough into pieces and to scrape stuck dough off your kneading surface.

Brotforms and bannetons: Some artisan bakers place their rising loaves in baskets made of coiled cane or willow branches called a brotform. This gives the finished loaves a pretty spiral pattern. Plastic versions are also available that are much easier to clean and maintain. French bannetons are linen-lined baskets used the same way. You can make a home-made banneton by lining a colander with a linen towel.

Dough scraper: A flexible plastic dough scraper is a rectangular spatula that is flat on one side and gently curved on the other. It is very useful for kneading wet artisan dough. I also use it to scoop proofed dough out of its bowl onto a floured kneading surface and to scrape dough bits off a presoaked mixing bowl before cleaning it with a sponge—the scraper wipes the bowl totally clean with little effort and prevents your sponge from being covered with sticky gluten.

Dough whisk: If you're mixing a big batch of dough by hand, a fork just doesn't cut it. A dough whisk has a loop-de-loop of sturdy wire that makes it easy to mix larger quantities.

Mixing bowls: It's useful to have several bowls of at least four-quart size made of stainless steel, glass, ceramic or plastic for mixing batter and proofing dough so that you can mix and proof more than one type of dough at the same time. Dough can even be kneaded directly in a bowl. Avoid aluminum and copper, which react chemically with the acids in sourdough.

Covers for mixing bowls and loaf pans: If you wish to avoid plastic wrap for environmental reasons, cover proofing starter or dough with dishes on top of proofing bowls, or overturned bowls or cooking pots over freeform loaves. Other options include sliding the proofing bowl into a re-used plastic bag or purchasing a clear acrylic proofing cover.

Non-stick or resistant kneading surface: While dough can be kneaded right inside the mixing bowl or on a smooth countertop, kneading is easier when the dough doesn't stick to the surface too easily. I prefer using a smooth, unfinished wooden cutting board. The wood resists sticking to the dough. You can also buy a silicone non-stick dough mat. If your cutting board tends to slide across your counter, try wetting a dish towel, wringing it out, then placing it flat against the counter beneath the cutting board.

Nylon basting brush: When making artisan bread you want to avoid adding too much flour to the dough. When dough is proofed on a floured surface, and then flipped over onto the kneading board for folding and shaping, I find it very useful to brush off the excess flour with a brush. The stiff, fine bristles are much better at whisking away flour than hands.

Parchment paper: To bake artisan loaves on a baking stone, place the dough on a sheet of parchment paper to allow easy transfer to the oven. Regular parchment is sold in supermarkets. Kitchen stores sell "super parchment" paper, a sturdy, indefinitely reusable alternative.

Step 2: Mixing the ingredients

Mixing evenly distributes the ingredients, hydrates the starch granules, activates enzymes that create flavor, and initiates gluten development. Stir in a circular motion to combine the bowl ingredients (at this point there should be no added flour). Next, vigorously mix a third to a half of the flour into the dough with a fork or dough whisk. Whisk in one direction only to align the gluten strands. Some bakers mix the dough a standard 100 times to make sure they are fully developing the gluten. I tend to mix for less time, until it becomes too difficult to mix with a fork. Slowly add additional flour until the dough becomes an elastic blob or shaggy mass, depending on the hydration level of the formula.

❖ Because of their lower gluten content, dough made with emmer, einkorn or triticale only needs mixing to combine and distribute the ingredients. True kneading is unnecessary.

❖ Pancakes and crêpes require just enough mixing to combine the ingredients.

Step 3: Kneading the dough

Kneading dough stretches, relaxes and realigns the gluten molecules into parallel, muscle-like fibers to create a three-dimensional web. Kneading also oxygenates the dough, providing oxygen for the microbes. If you are making artisan dough, don't knead in all the measured flour at this stage, because you'll need some of it during the folding and proofing stages later on.

Kneading dry doughs

Imitate this ancient Egyptian baker by placing your bowl of dough on the floor and knead right in the bowl while kneeling or sitting cross-legged. You'll gain greater leverage than is possible for people of average height kneading on a kitchen counter.

Americans are familiar with the physically demanding kneading of American pan breads and sweet doughs. These doughs, as well as bagel dough, are relatively dry and stiff. To knead dry dough, stretch it, fold it over on itself, and firmly press the two halves together with the heel of one or both hands. Make a quarter-turn of the dough between each folding. If possible, knead on a countertop that is lower than a kitchen counter to get the best leverage. Some bakers sit on the floor and knead the dough in the mixing bowl. Knead until the gluten is almost fully developed, 10–15 minutes.

Kneading wet doughs

Moderately wet artisan doughs are soft and sticky. They cannot be firmly kneaded because the dough will stick to the kneading surface and your hands. Instead, gently stretch artisan dough and fold it in half, then make a quarter-turn and stretch and fold it again. You can use a plastic dough scraper to flip the dough over

The French autolyse method

Some artisan bakers like to mix the flour and 90% of the water first, then let the mixture rest for 20–30 minutes before adding the rest of the ingredients. This resting time allows the starch to hydrate and initiates gluten development. This rest makes mixing and kneading much easier. Peter Reinhart's mash method described in the previous chapter is an outgrowth of the autolyse (AH-toe-leez) technique. In the times before electric mixers, autolyse was an easy way to handle large volumes of dough. Autolyse is especially important when baking with baker's yeast or small volumes of sourdough starter. If you use a high percentage of sourdough starter in your breads, as in this book, most of the flour has already been hydrated in the starter itself, making an autolyse unnecessary.

on itself without getting your fingers stuck to it, especially towards the beginning of the kneading process. Another way to stretch the dough is to pick it up and allow it to stretch downward through the force of gravity. Then drop the dough onto the board and flip it over on itself to fold it in half. Repeat process for a couple of minutes.

Halfway through the kneading process, you can rest for a couple of minutes and then finish. The resting time allows the gluten proteins to more fully hydrate and connect with one another, making the final minute of kneading easier. The dough will seem more "together" when you return; you'll be less tempted to add excess flour. Some gluten linkages break during resting, making the dough more extensible and leading to better oven spring (a last burst of rising detailed in chapter 9) and bigger holes in the crumb. If you've kneaded in too much flour, knead in one tablespoon of water at a time until the dough reaches the desired consistency.

Be careful to keep one side of the dough intact throughout the process by keeping the "good" side (the side with smooth outer "skin") down on the board; an intact gluten web is necessary to properly shape artisan dough. A torn surface will allow carbon dioxide to escape during proofing and will create an imperfect crust. Because artisan dough has an optimum hydration level, the gluten develops in only 3–5 minutes. You'll know the dough is done when it begins to form a cohesive blob. Properly kneaded dough has a smooth satiny appearance and an elastic texture. It will not tear easily when stretched using the window pane test. Doughs made with weak gluten flour cannot be stretched as far without tearing and must be handled more delicately.

The final stage of gluten development happens during the fermentation and proofing steps.

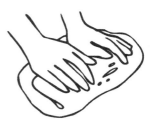

Gently stretch wet artisan dough (above), then fold it in half (below), press down lightly, and stretch and fold again until the dough becomes a smooth, elastic ball.

[Window pane test: to test the cohesiveness of a dough's gluten web, gently stretch a piece of dough thin enough to make it translucent to light. If it tears, the dough is not yet ready. Knead for another minute and test again]

Step 4: Shaping the dough

Shaping tightens the outer "skin," which is especially important when making artisan bread. Artisan dough that has not been properly shaped will spread out and flatten rather than puff up when baked.

A shaped ball of dough. The upper, "good" side should not have any tears in the skin.

Artisan and flatbread dough

If you are making freeform artisan loaves or flatbread dough, gently shape the dough into a ball in preparation for bulk fermentation: flour your hands, pick up the dough, turn the "good" side up. Gently and quickly pull the outer edges underneath, tucking the dough into the center. Rotate the ball as you do this so that it stretches evenly. Go around in a circle several times, until the gluten is stretched tight, but not so tight that it begins to tear. If it tears easily, it is probably not kneaded enough. When I am shaping a ball of dough I think of the shape of a mushroom cap.

Lightly flour the bottom of the bowl. Place the ball in the center of the bowl with the "good" side up. If you live in a dry climate, wet your hands and moisten the skin. Neither the bowl nor the surface is oiled. This is how you get a thick, crunchy artisan-style crust. Oil creates a thinner, softer crust. Cover the bowl with a lid, plate or plastic wrap.

Sweet dough

Shape the dough into a ball. If you live in a dry climate, wet your hands and moisten the skin. Lightly oil the dough with a neutral-flavored vegetable oil like canola oil, place it in a bowl and cover for bulk fermentation.

Doughs made with emmer, einkorn, triticale and rye must be placed into loaf pans after shaping because they do not contain enough gluten to hold their shape (chapter 5).

Sandwich dough

Shape the dough like sweet dough, but less tightly. Gently stretch the dough to fit the length of the loaf pan. Place the dough into a loaf pan that has been greased and sprinkled with semolina or cornmeal. To make a rounded top, leave as is. To make a flat top, flatten the dough evenly across the entire surface, including the corners. If you live in a dry climate, wet your hands and moisten the skin. In all climates, lightly oil the surface. Cover the loaf pan for proofing.

If you are making more than one loaf, let the dough rest 10 minutes on the kneading board, and then use a bench knife to divide the dough into separate loaves. You can weigh each piece for greater precision. Shape and place each loaf into its own pan.

Step 5: Bulk fermentation (first proof)

After the dough has been mixed and kneaded, it is given time to leaven. European artisan bakers refer to this step as bulk fermentation while American bakers call it the first proof. Pan breads only need a single proofing before baking, since they have no need to hold their shape. Proofing completes the development of the gluten, a process known as "ripening." By letting the dough sit undisturbed, the flour becomes more thoroughly hydrated. Additional gluten linkages form during this time.

In addition, the bubbles of carbon dioxide permeating through the dough stretch the gluten to create an optimal balance between elasticity and extensibility.

Medieval woodcut of peasants harvesting grain.

Never cover proofing dough with a moist towel. This does nothing to reduce evaporation; the crust will still dry out. Instead, protect proofing dough from moisture loss by covering the bowl with a pan lid or another bowl (if you wish to avoid plastic wrap).

Proofing temperatures and retardation

Sourdough breads are best fermented and proofed at room temperature (65–75°F/18–24°C). Temperatures above 90°F/32°C tend to foster the overgrowth of unwanted strains of bacteria that produce "off" flavors. It is also possible to retard any part of the fermentation and proofing process for several hours or even overnight by cooling or refrigerating the dough between 33°F/1°C and 50°F/10°C, a process known as retarding the dough. This option makes the process more flexible, making it easier to fit bread baking into your schedule. Higher fermentation temperatures lead to more lactic acid and less acetic acid; cooler temperatures encourage the bacteria that produce acetic acid. In addition, high temperatures lead to milder-flavored bread because the bacteria have less time to reproduce, while retarding the fermentation leads to much more richly-flavored sourdoughs.

Proofing times

Proofing times for sourdoughs vary according to the leavening power of the wild yeast. For example, Sourdoughs International's Russia culture only needs 1½ hours between kneading and baking. On the other hand, the San Francisco culture (which is notoriously slow) may need eight hours of bulk fermentation and three hours for proofing the loaves. Doughs made with ancient wheats or rye ferment more quickly than doughs made with common wheat due to the extra minerals in the flour.

Let the dough ferment until it has roughly doubled in size. I just eye it. You can also buy plastic proofing buckets with marked measurements on the side, or use masking tape to measure the doubling point on the side of the rising container. Try lightly poking the dough with your finger; if the indentation bounces back quickly, the dough is not fully proofed; if the indentation remains it is fully proofed. Another method is to make an incision in the top and take a look. Is the dough dotted with air bubbles or does it look dense and smooth? (It should contain air bubbles.) If the dough overproofs, gently knead it to de-gas it during Step 6.

Step 6: Folding and degassing the dough

In contrast to the American method of "punching down" the dough in between proofs, European artisan bakers treat their dough gently. Wet artisan breads are folded, degassed and shaped. Folding equalizes the dough temperature, redistributes the yeast and starch, strengthens the gluten, adds more oxygen, and creates a taught outer "skin" on freestanding loaves. Using this folding technique creates the open crumb characteristic of artisan breads in contrast to the tight, even crumb of American pan breads.

To use this method, lightly flour the kneading surface using some of the reserved flour. Use a plastic dough scraper to gently scoop the proofed dough out of the bowl onto the kneading surface, good side down. Gently stretch the dough in one direction, then fold it in thirds. Then turn the dough 90° and stretch and fold it again. If the dough seems under-kneaded at this point (i.e., the top surface tears too easily), do a little gentle kneading to tighten it up. Place the dough back in the bowl, moisten the surface with water if you live in a dry climate and cover for the second proof.

Folding artisan dough in thirds.

Step 7: Proofing the dough or rolling out

Artisan dough

Proof the dough a second time exactly as the first.

Sweet dough

Give the dough a bench rest at room temperature for at least 10–15 minutes (to allow the gluten to relax) before rolling it out and adding the filling. If you try to roll out the dough immediately, it will be very tight and will want to shrink back to its former shape. Let the dough rest as long as 30 minutes if that better fits your schedule. Then roll out the dough, add the filling, roll up and cut as directed in the formula. Moisten, oil or baste with melted Earth Balance™ or butter and cover for the final proof.

[Bench rest: A short period of rest for yeast dough that provides time for the gluten to relax]

[Earth Balance™ is a vegan, non-dairy, non-hydrogenated butter substitute available at natural food stores]

Flatbread

Allow the dough to rest for 10–15 minutes before rolling it out as directed in the formula.

Step 8: Second folding and final shaping

Fold and shape artisan dough a second time in preparation for a third and final proof.

Step 9: Final proof

The final artisan dough proof is done exactly like the first two proofs. If you will be baking artisan loaves directly on a baking stone or ceramic tiles, place the bread for its final rise on a sheet of parchment paper lining your baking peel to allow easy transfer to the oven. These instructions are explained in detail in the next chapter on artisan breads.

When to put proofed bread in the oven

Rising is an exponential process. It is very slow at first, then speeds up as the yeast population doubles, then doubles and doubles again. Therefore, it is especially important to watch the dough near the end of the final proof. When a loaf has proofed for the last (or only) time, it is ready to bake when it has roughly doubled in volume. To check the readiness, you can poke the dough with your finger: If the dough springs back, it is not yet ready. If the poke mark remains, the proofing is done.

❖ Underproofing results in a tight web that does not develop enough oven spring during baking.

❖ Overproofing weakens the gluten, causing the dough to lose its shape and flow outwards if it is not in a pan and to overrise and collapse in the oven.

❖ If you have an emergency, or forget to turn on the oven, retard the dough in the refrigerator (up to 12 hours). Fast-rising cultures may overproof during this time, but you can always lightly knead, reshape and reproof loaves later.

❖ **When in doubt, underproof. It leads to fewer problems than overproofing.**

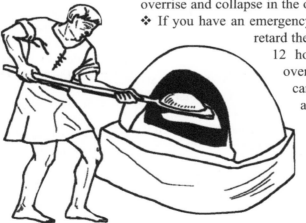

Roman slave putting proofed dough into a wood-fired earth oven (chapter 17).

Climatic considerations

I live in Arizona at 7,000 feet in altitude. I have found that high altitude has little effect on sourdough bread baking, but low humidity means you must be especially careful to retain moisture and prevent the skin of rising dough from drying out.

High altitude climates

In general, no special techniques are necessary for baking bread at high altitudes. While cakes and other airy, high-sugar baked goods have a tendency to lose their gas bubbles prematurely or collapse during baking, yeast breads are not vulnerable to these problems. Kneaded yeast breads have very strong gluten webs to trap the leavening gases.

❖ The low air pressure at high altitudes contributes to the easy expansion of rising bread dough, so be careful not to overproof dough before baking.

❖ Baked goods tend to brown faster at high altitudes than at sea level, so watch the crust development and turn down the oven temperature a little if it seems like the outside is browning faster than the inside is cooking (chapter 9).

Arid climates

❖ Many traditional dough formulas originated in humid climates. If you live in a dry climate, a dough may need less flour or more liquid to achieve the proper hydration level than mentioned in a formula or recipe. Base your decisions on the characteristics of the actual dough.

❖ If you mix a soaker for extra malt flavor using Peter Reinhart's method (p. 66), wrap it in plastic wrap or tightly pack into a plastic or glass storage container with no air space on top. This is the only way to prevent the skin from becoming crusty. The dough will not stick to the plastic wrap.

❖ After shaping dough for proofing, including after each folding or after the dough has been placed for its final proof on a piece of parchment paper or baking pan, I wet my hands and press them gently on the exposed dough surface to provide extra surface moisture. This step is especially important when making lean artisan doughs that are not oiled. You can also mist the dough with water using a spray bottle.

❖ After moistening with water, I oil sweet doughs and enriched sandwich breads with my hands or a nylon brush and then cover the baking pan with a tray or plastic wrap. You can also spray on a thin film of oil with a spray can designed for oil (ordinary spray bottles will clog up).

❖ It is important to spray European-style artisan loaves, including the slash marks, with warm water prior to baking and to create steam during the first few minutes of baking to prevent the skin from drying out. You'll learn about these steps in the next chapter.

❖ Making pita bread is especially easy in arid climates (p. 97). The surface of the dough must dry out for a few minutes before baking if it is to form an air pocket. This may be the reason why pita bread is a staple in the Middle East. On the other hand, if you want flatbread without a pocket, the surface must be moistened before baking.

9
Baking bread

"The smell of good bread baking, like the sound of lightly flowing water, is indescribable in its evocation of innocence and delight."
— M. F. K. Fisher, *The Art of Eating*

The basics: Those of us who are aficionados of artisan bread say that no other bread compares to artisan loaves baked directly on the floor of a wood-fired oven (chapter 17). Heat radiates from all sides of the interior, producing extraordinary oven spring and crust development. However, not everyone is lucky enough to have access to a real bread oven. To mimic the radiant heat of an earth or brick hearth oven, you'll need a baking stone or unglazed quarry tiles.

Introduction to baking bread

Baking bread is easy. Here's the basic outline for baking artisan bread (the details are provided in this chapter): when the dough is fully proofed and ready to bake, gently transfer the dough to your baking peel (if the last proof was not done on the peel itself), slash one or more cuts across the surface and then use a spray bottle to mist the surface with water. Open the oven door all the way, grab the peel handle and shove the peel into the oven. With a quick jerking motion, slide the dough and parchment directly onto the center of the stone and close the door. A few seconds later, open the door and pour about ½ cup water into a cast iron skillet pre-positioned in the oven. Close the door to prevent the eruption of steam from scalding you or escaping from the oven. A minute or so later, add a second round of steam. If you are baking artisan bread you may need to lower the oven temperature one or more times after the bread is placed in the oven. When the bread is finished baking, remove it from the oven and place it on a cooling rack (remove it from the loaf pan if necessary). When the bread has reached room temperature, you can slice it (hot bread is still cooking — prematurely slicing it will produce a gummy crumb). That's it!

Using a baking stone or ceramic tiles

Place a baking stone (see definition on next page) or center ceramic tiles on the center of an oven rack. Place the rack either in the center of the oven or toward the top. The idea is to capture radiant heat from all surfaces of the oven. Place the second rack directly underneath the first. Place a small cast iron skillet in the front to one side or the other. You'll be pouring water into the skillet to create steam.

I leave my ceramic tiles and cast iron skillet in my oven all the time. They do not interfere with other baking needs. While extra energy is initially required to heat up the tiles and skillet, they help to retain heat and maintain an even oven temperature.

When baking artisan bread on a baking stone, preheat the oven for 30 minutes to an hour before baking. Because much of the heat for baking the bread will radiate up into the loaf from the stone, you want the oven heat to fully penetrate the stone before the dough is slid onto it.

❖ European artisan breads and Middle Eastern and Asian flatbreads are baked at high temperatures (400–600°F/204–316°C). Artisan breads need high heat to produce their signature thick, dark crusts and resulting flavors.

❖ Because pan breads do not require high radiant heat, the oven need only barely reach baking temperature before baking. Pan breads and sweet breads are baked at moderate temperatures (350–400°F/177–204°C) until lightly browned.

❖ Large loaves are baked at a lower temperature and for a longer time than small breads to allow the loaf interior to cook fully before the crust gets too dark.

Baking tools

Baker's peel: If baking free-standing artisan loaves, you'll need a baker's peel, a paddle with a long handle designed for transferring bread onto a baking stone (see historical illustration at right). Peels come in different sizes, from small enough for a single loaf to larger sizes designed for large pizzas or multiple loaves. Some peels are aluminum and have a wooden handle. These are easiest to use because the thinness of the aluminum allows the dough to slide off the end onto the hearth stone very easily. Some peels are made of a solid piece of wood. In a pinch, turn over a baking sheet and place the dough on the backside.

Baking stone: A ceramic slab placed on your oven rack to provide a hearth-like baking surface—a necessity for baking crusty artisan bread. Choose a stone that fits in your oven. There should be at least 2" of space around all four sides of the stone to allow air circulation. Don't bother with the cheap, thin, light-weight versions now so readily available—they won't provide the necessary heat storage. If, like me, you can't afford a professional grade baking stone, buy unglazed ceramic tiles from a flooring supplier. I have twelve 6" wide, ½" thick tiles stacked in a double (1" thick) layer, creating a 12" x 18" baking surface. The tiles cost me 50 cents each. Another more expensive option is the HearthKit™ Oven Insert, which has a one inch-thick base stone and two removable sides that radiate additional heat into the bread, like the side walls of a hearth oven. An alternative to a baking stone is a La Cloche™ covered clay baker, which holds in the steam released by the bread, removing the need for another way to create steam. A cast iron Dutch oven (plain or enameled) is a good substitute for a La Cloche™, but not necessarily cheaper.

Cooling rack: Bread develops the best texture when properly cooled before slicing. A cooling rack allows air to circulate underneath your loaves.

Dough razor: Use a curved sharp dough razor (*lame*—"lahm"—in French) available at kitchen stores to make clean slashes on the tops of artisan breads with the middle of the blade without tearing the delicate dough on the ends of the blade before baking. A sharp serrated bread knife is a good substitute.

Instant-read thermometer: If you are unsure of your ability to tell when a loaf is done baking, insert a probe thermometer into the center of the loaf. "Instant-read" thermometers actually take about 30 seconds to register the temperature.

Kitchen timer: I like to multitask while baking bread. I carry my timer around with me, allowing me to free my mind for other things while waiting for dough to proof or bake. Timers come in battery-powered and non-electric spring-powered versions.

Oven mitts: Buy two! Artisan breads are baked at very hot (500°F/260°C) or higher) temperatures. Get protection up to the elbow if possible. It may take some searching. I prefer plain cloth. Cheap oven mitts and silicone mitts are generally too short to create much protection. Silicone mitts melt above 450–500°F (232–260°C).

Oven thermometer: Many home ovens have inaccurate oven thermostats. Buy a simple oven thermometer and hang it at the center of your oven to test and calibrate the thermostat.

Small cast iron skillet: Place a 6" cast iron skillet (mine is enameled) or stainless steel cake pan in your oven on a lower shelf or the oven floor near the door. You will pour water or ice cubes into it to produce steam for artisan breads.

Spray bottle: Fill an ordinary plastic spray bottle with water (found in the kitchen section of a supermarket or a hardware store) for misting your dough before putting it in the oven.

19th century book illustration.

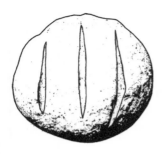

Slashing and docking

When bread is baked, water in the dough turns to steam and rapidly expands. Slashing or scoring artisan crust or "docking" flatbread (poking it with a fork) controls the release of the steam.

Don't worry — slashed dough will not deflate unless it is overproofed. The air cells in the dough are not connected to each other.

To slash a loaf, use a very sharp razor (*lame*). Use the center of the blade to make clean cuts ¼–½ inch deep. Avoid tearing the dough with the ends of the blade. Properly proofed dough will not deflate when slashed because the gluten web is composed of closed cells. However, slashing can deflate overproofed dough.

Slash patterns can be individualized to express your creativity. Make single slashes, crosses and complex hatching patterns as desired. The more slashes, the more difficult to avoid tearing, especially if two or more slashes cross over one another. If you use a shared community wood-fired oven (chapter 17), do what people used to do in such circumstances and let everyone choose their own "branding" pattern so that it is easy to tell whose loaves are whose after they are baked.

Artisan bread

For round or oval free form loaves, hold the blade vertically. For thinner, oval loaves, you can also hold the blade at about 30° off horizontal; when baked the edge of the cut will form a crunchy "ear." Artisan "country loaves" are baked without slashing to produce a natural, random burst pattern in the crust.

A few examples of branding patterns for round and torpedo-shaped bâtards.

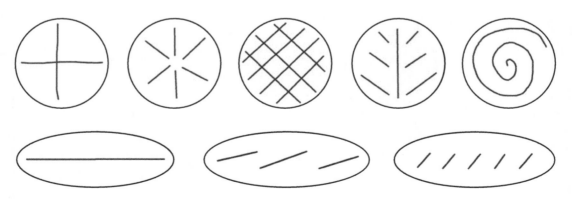

Pan bread

Slashing is not required. Because pan breads and sweet breads are baked at moderate temperatures, so the steam escapes from the bread at a lower rate. Many bakers slash pan breads anyway for decorative purposes. Make a single slash down the center of the loaf or a series of angled slashes across the width of the loaf.

Flatbread

Flatbreads and prebaked pizza crusts, with the exception of pita bread, are "docked" (poked) with a fork or a rolling docker or docker stamp available at kitchen stores to make a series of small holes that serve a similar function as slashing. The holes allow the internal steam to escape from the bread. Undocked pita bread puffs up into a ball because the outer surface quickly dries out and forms a skin that prevents the escape of steam. You don't want large flatbreads and pizza crusts to turn into giant pita pockets.

Baking bread

The importance of steam

Steam keeps the dough surface moist for as long as possible to allow greater expansion of the dough before the crust hardens. Steam also provides more time for enzymes to create browning reactions in the crust. Steam produces a chewier, darker crust that is essential to artisan bread. The browning of the crust comes from two sources: at lower temperatures, the Maillard reaction joins amino acids (protein fragments) with sugars. At even higher temperatures, sugars caramelize. It is these reactions that create the "baking bread aroma" of yeast breads. As explained earlier in the book, sourdough breads have more of that special aroma because the yeast and bacteria create more protein and sugar fragments to brown during baking.

❖ To reproduce the effect of commercial steam injectors, mist lean artisan loaves and flat breads with hot water before baking. Place the loaves into the oven, then pour ½ cup water into your pre-heated cast iron skillet; the water will instantly vaporize. In another minute or two, pour in a second ½ cup water.

[Steam: Vaporized water at or above the boiling point]

[Maillard reaction: A complex series of browning reactions between carbohydrates and proteins caused by heating]

[Caramelization: The process whereby sugar is heated until it oxidizes (burns). Caramelization begins around 310°F/ 154°C. It produces more than 100 aromatic, sweet, sour, and bitter compounds]

Shut the door as quickly as possible to seal in the steam.

❖ Some people prefer the ice cube method; pour 1cup ice cubes into the skillet; the ice cubes sublimate directly to steam.

❖ When properly proofed dough is placed in a hot oven, it rapidly expands for one last time in a process called oven spring. Oven spring adds 10–33% to the volume of a loaf. Many people mistakenly believe that oven spring comes from a final, rapid growth of yeast producing CO_2 bubbles. However, most of the expansion actually comes from the sudden production of steam from the alcohol and water in the dough. In addition, air in the dough expands in volume.

Medieval woman shoveling hot coals out of a brick, wood-fired oven in preparation for baking.

Baking temperatures

❖ To mimic the effects of a real wood-fired oven, I like to place artisan dough in a very hot oven and then reduce the temperature a couple of times during baking (read about wood-fired ovens in chapter 17). This method produces excellent oven spring and a crunchy crust, yet provides time for the insides to fully cook without burning the crust.

❖ Experience will teach you how to tell when the bread is finished baking by looking at the crust. A fully baked loaf has a hollow sound when tapped on the bottom with your fingers. You can also insert an instant-read thermometer thermometer into the center of the loaf. A fully cooked loaf reaches 190–210°F (88–99°C) in the center (lower for pan loaves and sweet breads, higher for artisan bread).

Which is better: electric or gas ovens?

Some people prefer electric ovens over gas ovens for baking artisan breads because the dry, steady, even heat creates the best conditions for radiant heat transfer. If you have an electric oven with a convection setting, turn it off when baking artisan bread—the convection currents prevent radiant heat transfer. Sweet doughs and American-style pan breads don't need radiant heat (although it won't hurt them) because they have softer, thinner crusts, so convection ovens work fine for baking them.

Cooling and slicing bread

Small breads and flat breads, which have a high ratio of crust to crumb, are best eaten warm. All other breads should be placed on a cooling rack to allow air circulation under the loaf. When a properly-baked loaf of artisan bread is taken out of the oven, the crust shrinks, producing audible crackles, and creating fine cracks.

❖ Never cut into a loaf (pan or artisan) until at least 30 minutes after it comes out of the oven. The ideal is about two hours. Why the wait? During baking, the wheat proteins coagulate when the interior of the loaf reaches 140°F (60°C). When this happens, the loaf can expand no further. At this point, the proteins release water that is immediately absorbed by starch granules that burst open in the heat. The starch and water form a gel, the way cornstarch thickens gravy. Then the bread is removed from the oven and the cooling process begins. As the bread cools, the starch stiffens to form the structure of the bread. Prematurely sliced bread will have a gummy crumb.

At potlucks I like to give bread-slicing demonstrations to avoid watching my beautiful artisan bread get compacted into a dense lump.

❖ To slice crusty artisan bread, which is hard on the outside but delicate on the inside, use a serrated bread knife. Saw lightly back and forth to slice the crust without squashing the interior.

❖ If your bread is denser than expected, slice it very thin and toast it—the way dense whole rye breads are traditionally eaten.

Storing sourdough bread

Sourdough bread will store without molding for at least a week at room temperature due to the natural preservatives produced by the lactic acid bacteria (chapter 2). Staling involves both drying and the crystallization of starch molecules in the crust and crumb.

❖ Bread will stay fresher if stored in a dry, cool location.

❖ Small breads and breads with a high ratio of crust to crumb will stale faster than large loaves with lots of interior crumb.

❖ Lean artisan breads stale faster than enriched breads that contain fat and sugar. Enriched breads inhibit staling because the fat and sugar interfere with the crystallization process.

❖ To maintain a crisp artisan crust, leave the bread uncovered for up to 24 hours. Keep the cut edge of an artisan loaf protected by storing the bread vertically with the cut side down.

Refrigeration speeds up the staling process, so I recommend not storing bread in the refrigerator unless you live in a hot climate without air-conditioning.

❖ Beyond 24 hours, store artisan bread in a ventilated bread box or wrap loaves in cotton or linen towels. If you live in an arid climate, plastic bags are OK, too

❖ You can temporarily "refresh" bread by warming it in a moderate oven (350°F/177°C) for about 20 minutes. The starch crystals will temporarily dissolve, but will recrystallize once the bread cools down again. See chapter 16 for more ideas on what to do with stale bread.

Medieval woodcut of woman selling bread.

Part III
Sourdough breads

"Of all smells, bread; of all tastes, salt."
— George Herbert

10
Artisan breads

"If thou tastest a crust of bread, thou tastest all the stars and all the heavens."
— Robert Browning

The basics: This chapter explains how to make lean, wet artisan dough that I use to make free-form artisan loaves, pan loaves, Mediterranean and Asian flatbreads, pizza crust, pita bread and more. Also included are recipes for no-knead Italian ciabatta and focaccia. Later chapters will explain how to use this artisan dough to make sourdough tortillas and English muffins. Read chapter 11 to learn about adding cracked grains, fruit, vegetables, herbs and spices to bread dough.

❧ Basic artisan dough ❧

This is a 100% whole wheat, 75% hydration European artisan bread formula that works well with either hard wheat or spelt. This hydration level is necessary to create a dough with the same hydration characteristics as a 65–67% hydration dough made with 100% unbleached flour. If you choose to mix whole wheat and unbleached flours, use an in-between hydration percentage (i.e., if you use a 50/50 mixture, use a 70% hydration level). The formula uses 20 oz sourdough starter to make 29.5 oz (1¾ lb) dough, enough to make one 1 lb loaf of baked bread. Scale the formula as desired to make multiple loaves using the baker's percentage system. To get a feel for how hydration affects bread texture and crust development, experiment with slightly wetter and drier doughs by adding or subtracting 1–2 tablespoons (½–1oz/14–28 grams) of water.

Dough

Ingredient	U.S. Weight	U.S. Volume	Metric
Culture	20 oz	1⅞ cups	567 g
Flour	6.7 oz	1⅓ cups	190 g
Water	2.5 oz	Scant ⅓ cup	71 g
Salt	0.3 oz	1.5 teaspoons	8 g

Baker's formula	
Flour	100%
Water	75%
Salt	1.8%
Total	*176.8%*

1. Activate culture (chapter 4). After returning 8 oz to the storage jar, there will be 20 oz left for use in formula.
2. Weigh water and salt into bowl. Weigh flour in separate bowl.
3. Mix water, salt and about 2 oz flour into culture. Reserve another 2 oz flour for use during proofing and folding.
4. Use some of the remaining 2 oz flour to dust kneading surface. Turn dough out onto kneading surface and gently knead the rest of that 2 oz into the dough for 3–5 minutes using the artisan method described in chapter 10, giving the dough a brief rest in the middle of kneading.
5. Use some of the reserved flour to dust the proofing bowl. Shape dough into ball and place good (unbroken skin) side up into bowl. If you live in a dry climate, wet your hands and moisten the skin of the dough.
6. Cover bowl and proof until dough is doubled in bulk.
7. Follow shaping and proofing directions for the desired type of bread (see below).
8. Preheat oven to 550°F (288°C) for 30 minutes–1 hour.

Crust or crumb?

Which do you like better, thick crunchy artisan-style crust, or fluffy, moist crumb? If it's the crust you want, choose a bread with a high ratio of surface area to interior.

❖ The best breads for crust-lovers include small breads and fougasse (see below). Thin, small artisan breads are also the best choice if you want to serve bread right out of the oven. Because crunchy artisan crust dries out and goes stale, if you leave it exposed to the air, or becomes soft if you wrap it, crusty breads are best eaten within 24 hours.

❖ If you want lots of soft crumb, make a round freeform boule or torpedo-shaped bâtard. Larger loaves must cool for at least 30 minutes–2 hours before the crumb is fully set. Round loaves will keep for a week or two, although the crust will soften when wrapped.

❖ Flatbreads have their own special texture, neither crunchy nor fluffy, but soft and puffy and good for wrapping foods or scooping up thick stews.

Folding artisan dough in thirds.

Making freeform loaves

These are the basic peasant-style artisan bread shapes. After bulk fermentation, use a plastic dough scraper to turn the dough out onto the floured kneading board, good side down. Brush off excess flour with a nylon pastry brush. Gently stretch and fold the dough in thirds, turn the dough 90° and stretch and fold into thirds again. If the dough seems under-kneaded at this point (i.e., the top surface tears too easily), do a little gentle kneading and shaping to tighten it up. Place dough back in bowl, moisten surface with water (if you live in a dry climate) and cover for the second proof. Fold and shape as explained below for the third and final proof. Slash as desired before baking.

To bake freeform loaves, reduce temperature to 500°F (260°C). Mist loaf with water and slide onto baking stone. Pour ½ cup water into the cast iron skillet and close oven; repeat in one minute. Bake 15–20 minutes until the side facing the back of the oven begins to brown. I remove the parchment paper at this point. Turn the loaf around and bake another 15–20 minutes until the loaf is a rich, deep brown, but not burnt. If the crust seems to be darkening too rapidly, reduce temperature to 450°F (232°C) to allow the inside to bake fully. Cool bread on cooling rack.

Round boules

A boule ("ball" in French) is an easy shape to make. After the second proof, shape into a ball, cut a piece of parchment paper and set the parchment on the peel. Place dough on parchment. If you live in a dry climate, wet your hands and moisten the dough. Cover dough with an overturned pot or bowl and proof until doubled. Slash loaf as desired. Bake as directed above.

[Boulangerie: French word for bakery, derived from the word "boule"]

Brotform boules

A variation of the boule involves proofing the ball in a coiled brotform basket to produce a concentric circle design. For the last proof, generously coat inner surface of brotform with flour to prevent dough from sticking. Place shaped dough good side down in basket, cover and proof. When ready to bake, turn over the peel and place it on top of basket. Flip over basket and gently remove from dough. Slash if desired and bake as directed above.

Bâtards

Bâtards are torpedo-shaped ovals. During the last shaping, shape the dough into a ball and give the ball a 15–20 minute bench rest to relax the gluten. Place dough good side down. Gently stretch and fold dough into thirds. Gently stretch dough to make an oval. Make two small folds on each end to taper the ends. Place right side up on the parchment for the final proof. Use a baker's couche (p. 72) if desired to ensure that the loaf keeps its shape. Make several 45° slashes across the width of the loaf and bake.

Making small breads

These breads can be eaten soon after coming out of the oven. One bulk fermentation period is enough. For greater flavor development, shape and proof the dough twice before baking.

"Pillow" bread

This is a super-easy, rustic bread. It has a crunchy crust and a light, fluffy interior. After bulk fermentation, turn dough good side down onto a floured surface and gently stretch the bread a bit. Avoid deflating the air bubbles in the dough as much as possible. Use a bench knife to cut 2–4" square or triangular "pillows" out of the dough (for a total of 6–12). Try to make them roughly the same size for even baking. Arrange pieces on the parchment for final proof, leaving at least two inches between each pillow to allow room for expansion. Reduce oven temperature to 450°F (232°C). Bake 15–20 minutes, until crust is golden brown.

Round rolls

After bulk fermentation, use a bench knife to divide dough into individual rolls (4 oz rolls are standard, in which case you'll get seven). Shape each roll into a ball as if making a tiny boule. Place on parchment for final proof. For a crunchy crust, reduce oven temperature to 450°F (232°C) and bake 15–20 minutes, until crust is a golden, dark brown. For soft crust, reduce temperature to 375°F (191°C) and bake 20 minutes, until lightly browned.

Twisted bread sticks

After the bulk fermentation, use a bench knife to divide dough into 12–24 individual pieces. Roll each piece into a rope ½–1" wide, as if you were rolling a clay coil. For seasoned breadsticks, roll the coils in kosher salt, sesame seeds or poppy seeds. Hold onto each end of the rope and twist ends in opposite directions a few times. Place on parchment for the final proof. Reduce oven temperature to 450°F (232°C). Bake about 10 minutes, or until crust is a golden, dark brown.

Flatbreads from India to Italy

Simple flatbread

Versions of this basic baked flatbread can be found all over the world. In India, flatbread is called naan. Flatbreads work well with up to 50% non-wheat flours. For example, Tibetan barley bread includes toasted barley flour mixed with wheat. Chapter 12 explains how to cook these breads in a stovetop skillet (Sourdough wraps).

After the bulk fermentation, use a bench knife to divide the dough into pieces or pinch off lumps by hand. Use your hands or a rolling pin to flatten each piece into a round ⅛–¼" thick. Place the rounds on a parchment-lined peel or large baking sheet. Mist the surfaces with water to prevent a pita pocket from forming. You can also dock (pierce) the surfaces with a fork, but if the bread surface is wet enough this isn't usually necessary. At this point, the rounds can be baked immediately, or, for extra-puffy bread, the dough can be covered and proofed (until it doubles in volume) before baking. Try it both ways to see which version you prefer. Slide breads off the peel onto a baking stone or place the entire baking sheet in the oven. Bake for about 5 minutes, or until you start to see a few brown spots appear on the surfaces. Serve while warm and pliable or wrap in cloth or plastic to keep their softness. Indian naan is brushed with garlic ghee (clarified butter) as soon as it comes out of the oven. Earth Balance™ makes a good vegan substitute.

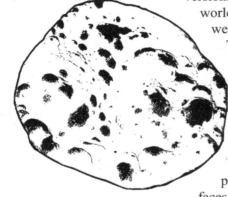

Indian naan. Naan is traditionally baked in a tandoor oven, a wood-fired oven found from the eastern Mediterranean to India. The vertical oven walls have a conical shape. Flatbreads are slapped onto the vertical walls to bake.

Pita pockets

Pita bread is found throughout the Arab and Muslim countries of the Middle East and Central Asia. The flatbread is allowed to puff naturally in the oven to form an air pocket that is perfect for stuffing. The trick to making pita dough form a balloon of air inside is to dry the surface before baking. During baking, steam cannot escape through the skin, so it expands to form a pocket. Traditional pita formulas include 1 teaspoon of sugar or other sweetener, but it's not absolutely necessary. Twenty eight oz dough will make 12 medium pitas, 6 large pitas, or 24 small pitas. You can even make mini-pitas 1½" across for appetizers!

Pita bread is super easy for beginners yet looks dramatically difficult.

Use a bench knife to divide the dough into individual pitas.

After the bulk fermentation, use a bench knife to divide dough into individual pieces (the dough can also be wrapped in plastic and stored in a refrigerator for a day or two before rolling out). On a lightly floured surface, use a rolling pin to roll each piece into a circle about ⅛-inch thick. Set each round aside uncovered on a floured surface for a few minutes before baking. Slide one or more rounds at a time onto the baking stone and close the oven (no steam). The breads will begin to puff almost immediately. Bake for a few minutes. Remove each pita before it begins to brown—you want the crust to remain pliable. Place the pitas on a tray to cool for a few minutes before serving. Cover them with a towel or place in a plastic bag to keep them from drying out. As they cool, they will deflate. Keep pitas tightly wrapped if they will not be served immediately.

Central Asian naan

Central Asian naan is an artisan dough moistened with milk or yogurt rather than water. Jeffrey Alford and Naomi Duguid write in *Flatbreads & Flavors* that one common variety of naan found among the Muslim Uighurs of China's far western Taklimakan Desert is rolled out into a large pizza-like bread. The middle of the bread is pricked or stamped with a decorative bread stamp (use a fork or make a stamp by pounding nails through a small piece of wood in a decorative design) while the rim is left thick like pizza crust. When baked (traditionally in a tandoor oven) the rim puffs up while the center remains flat.

The bread is traditionally sprinkled with cumin seeds, sliced scallions and salt before baking.

French fougasse

Fougasse (ladder bread) often contains chopped fresh Italian herbs and sliced brine-cured olives. A similar bread sprinkled with nigella is found in Afghanistan, Iran and Turkey. After the bulk fermentation, turn the dough out onto a floured surface and stretch to make an oval of the desired thickness and place on a parchment-lined peel (try ¾" thick and see how you like it). Using a sharp paring knife, make a series of parallel slits across the width of the dough about 1–1½" apart. Gently stretch the dough to open the slits. You can also make other slash designs such as a sheaf of wheat or a pinwheel. To make the Central Asian version, use your fingers to dimple the surface; gently stretch the bread to open the holes.

Italian focaccia

The original Roman *panis focacius* was a flatbread cooked in the ashes of an open fire ("focus" is the Latin word for hearth and "panis" means bread). Today, focaccia (foe-CAT-cha) is as varied as Italy itself. It can be thick or thin, plain or topped with olive oil, herbs and seeds, made from artisan dough or very wet dough (see "No-knead focaccia" below), and even sliced horizontally to make sandwiches.

[Nigella (*Nigella sativa*): Known as black caraway, black cumin, *kalonji* (Indian) and *swartzcummel* (German), the small, tear-shaped seeds have an aromatic flavor reminiscent of black pepper, but without the heat. Mohammed says in the Koran, "Use this Black seed, it has a cure for every disease except death." Available at Indian and Middle Eastern grocery stores.

After the bulk fermentation, hand-stretch and press the dough to the desired thickness, (try ½–1" thick) and place on parchment-lined peel. If desired, use your fingers to dimple the surface. Make the dimples roughly ½" deep and 1" apart. The indentations are perfect for holding drizzled olive oil and other toppings like fresh chopped rosemary or sautéed onions. Cover and proof until doubled. Just before baking, use a pastry brush to lightly brush the surface with olive oil (or use canola oil or melted Earth Balance™). If you want toppings, sprinkle them on the dough at this time. Bake 15–20 minutes until crust is browned as desired.

Other bread shapes

Sourdough calzones/turnovers

After the bulk fermentation, divide dough into 16 pieces. Roll each piece into a circle about ⅛-inch thick. Spoon a couple of tablespoons of filling in the center of the dough. Fold the circle over on itself to form a half-moon shape. Crimp the edges with your fingers or the tines of a fork. Moisten the dough with water or oil and place on parchment-lined peel or an oiled baking sheet, cover, and let rise about 30 minutes–1 hour, depending on how fast your sourdough culture proofs. Bake at 375°F (191°C) until the calzones are lightly browned.

Pan bread and sweet rolls

Lean artisan dough can also be baked in a loaf pan like American pan breads or used to make sweet rolls in place of sweet dough. See the next chapter for directions on proofing and baking sandwich bread and sweet rolls.

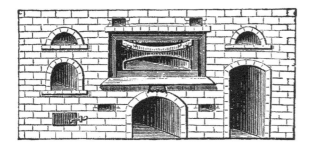

❧ Pizza crust ❧

Baker's formula	
Flour	100%
Water	75%
Salt	1.8%
Total	*176.8%*

You can use the basic artisan dough as described on page 93 to make one 16" deep dish pizza crust or two thinner crusts. I prefer to make one medium-crust 16" pizza, so I've developed the following formula to make a smaller amount of dough. You could also use this formula to make two 16" thin crust pizzas.

Dough

Ingredient	U.S. Weight	U.S. Volume	Metric
Culture	16 oz	1½ cups	454 g
Flour	4 oz	1 cup	113 g
Water	1 oz	2 tablespoons	28 g
Salt	0.22 oz	1¼ teaspoons	6 g

1. To make 16 oz active starter without any waste, feed the starter 1.5 oz each flour and water at each of the three activation feedings (⅜ cup flour and 3 tablespoons water). Put 8 oz starter (¾ cup) back into the starter jar.

2. Follow artisan dough directions through bulk fermentation.

3. Flip dough out onto floured surface and use rolling pin to roll out a 16" crust, or stretch and pull by hand for a rustically-textured crust (whole wheat dough is not suited for tossing; it tears). Fold the crust over the rolling pin to help transfer it to a peel or pizza pan and unroll it into place.

4. If you live in a dry climate, wet your hands and moisten the dough surface. Wherever you live, pour a tablespoon of oil into your hands and spread across the dough. Cover with plastic wrap and proof until doubled.

5. Place pizza pan in oven and bake 10 minutes at 550°F (288°C). You can also slide the crust directly onto the baking stone if the stone is wide enough for the dough. Remove crust from oven. Add toppings and bake another 10 minutes or until done.

6. Cool on a cooling rack for 20 minutes before slicing.

Pizza sauce

This is my favorite pizza sauce. It makes enough for one large 16" pizza. It freezes well. The secret ingredient is the fennel.

1 tablespoon olive or canola oil
5–7 cloves minced garlic
1 teaspoon whole fennel seeds
2 6-oz cans tomato paste
1 tablespoon dried flaked oregano or Italian herb mixture
Salt to taste

1. Sauté the garlic and fennel in the oil over medium heat for a few minutes, until garlic is just barely cooked.
2. Mix the sauté with the remaining ingredients.

❧ Ciabatta ☙

If you increase the hydration of whole wheat artisan dough to 85% (change to 75% if using unbleached flour), you create a very wet dough perfect for Italian ciabatta. Ciabatta (chi-BAH-tuh) is a thick flatbread that means "slipper" in Italian. During the long fermentation time, the gluten becomes well developed, creating a very stretchy dough. The super-wet hydration creates large, irregular holes in the crumb. A long fermentation time allows the gluten to form without kneading and creates lots of sourdough flavor. Extra flour not included in the formula is necessary to prevent the wet dough from sticking to the kneading surface. To make focaccia or pizza crust with this formula, simply flatten or roll out the dough to the desired thickness.

Baker's formula

Flour	100%
Water	85%
Salt	1.8%
Oil	0.5%
Total	*191.8%*

Dough

Ingredient	U.S. Weight	U.S. Volume	Metric
Culture	20 oz	1⅛ cups	567 g
Flour	6 oz	1½ cups	170 g
Water	0.6 oz	4½ tablespoons	102 g
Salt	0.3 oz	1½ teaspoons	8 g
Olive oil (optional)	0.3 oz	1 tablespoon	9 g

Ciabatta proofed for 18 hours to hydrate the gluten and create a very stretchy dough.

1. Combine starter with rest of ingredients. Mix briefly with your fingers. Cover bowl and proof 18 hours.
2. Generously flour kneading surface. Use a plastic dough scraper to scoop dough onto floured surface. Dust top with more flour. Gently stretch and flatten dough, being careful to avoid too much degassing. Fold dough into thirds, turn 90°, and fold in thirds a second time to produce a square mound. Cover and bench rest for 15 minutes.
3. Use bench knife to divide dough into two pieces. Stretch each ciabatta into an oblong rectangle about 1½" thick and place side-by-side, good side up, on a parchment-lined peel or baking sheet. Cover and proof until doubled.
4. Preheat oven to 500°F (260°C). Slide dough off peel or place baking tray in oven. Add steam to the oven as for regular artisan bread. Turn down temperature to 450°F (232°C). Bake 25–30 minutes. Flip over and bake another 5–10 minutes until surface is lightly browned.

❧ No-knead focaccia ☙ & pizza crust

If you increase the hydration of artisan dough to 100%, you create a batter dough that is essentially active sourdough starter. Because the batter cannot hold its shape, it is baked in a cast iron skillet or muffin pan. If desired, add fresh chopped or dried herbs to the batter. Don't weight it down with too many heavy ingredients. To make no-knead pizza, pre-bake the crust in a large cast iron skillet, cool to room temperature, then add toppings and bake again until toppings are cooked.

Baker's formula

Flour	100%
Water	100%
Salt	1.8%
Oil	1.5%
Total	203.3%

Dough

Ingredient	U.S. Weight	U.S. Volume	Metric
Culture	13 oz	Scant 1½ cup	40 g
Flour	1.5 oz	⅛ cup	43 g
Water	1.5 oz	3 tablespoons	43 g
Salt	0.3 oz	1½ teaspoons	8 g
Olive oil	0.1 oz	1 teaspoon	3 g

1. To make 13 oz active starter activate the starter with two feedings of 1.5 oz each flour and water. Save 8 oz to put back in the starter jar.

2. For the third feeding, which also doubles as the ingredient mixing step, add the remaining flour, water, salt and olive oil. Stir in one direction until combined. Cover bowl and proof until doubled in bulk.

3. Oil the skillet, baking sheet or muffin pan and dust with semolina. Use a rubber spatula to gently pour the batter into the skillet or pan, being careful to prevent as much deflation as possible. If desired, gently brush the surface with olive oil. Cover pan and proof until doubled in bulk. Preheat oven to 500°F (260°C). After putting pan in oven, lower temperature to 400°F (204°C). Bake 15–35 minutes, depending on size and thickness of the bread, until crust becomes a crispy golden brown.

Woodcut from The Assyse of Bread, *early 16th century. "Here begynnethe the boke named the assyse of bread what it ought to waye after the pryce of a quarter of wheete. And also thassyse of al maner of wood, lathe, bourde, tymbre, and the waight of butyre, and chese. Enprynted at the request of Mychaell Englysshe and Iohn Rudstone aldermen of the cyte of London."*

11
Enriched breads

"What was the best thing before sliced bread?"
— George Carlin

The basics: Enriched breads contain fat, sugar and other ingredients and are usually baked in pans. Because fat and sugar cause bread to brown more quickly, enriched breads are baked at a lower temperature than lean artisan breads. In this chapter, you'll learn how to make American-style sandwich bread, crackers, sweet dough and enriched batter breads.

Extra ingredients and how they affect dough

Sugar

Sugar adds flavor to pan breads and sweet doughs. A little sugar speeds up fermentation by providing instant food for the yeast. A lot of sugar slows down fermentation because it dehydrates the yeast. Liquid sweeteners like agave nectar and maple syrup increase the dough hydration level. Reduce the water content as necessary to maintain the desired dough consistency. Adding sugar to bread dough increases the amount of caramelization, producing a darker crust. For this reason, enriched doughs are baked at a moderate temperature to avoid burning.

Fat

Fat from any source, such as vegetable oils, nut butters and animal fats, lubricates strands of gluten, shortening them. A shortened gluten web produces a rich, tender crumb but also makes the web more prone to tearing. Bread containing fat retains more moisture than lean artisan breads, which slows the staling process. When added in small amounts, different kinds of fats are interchangeable. I like to use ground flax seeds for a healthy dose of omega-3 fats. Count liquid vegetable oil as part of the dough hydration percentage.

The origin of the term "shortening" was as a synonym for baking fat.

[Omega-3s: Poly-unsaturated fatty acids found in leafy greens, vegetable oils, and deep ocean fish that have beneficial health effects]

Milk and yogurt

Dairy and non-dairy milks contain fat and sugar and produce a tender crumb. Many Middle Eastern and Central Asian flat-breads are moistened with yogurt rather than water. Live cultured milk products are scalded before adding to yeast dough so that the lactobacteria do not interfere with the sourdough culture.

Flavored liquids

Broths, juices and other liquids can be used in place of water to hydrate a dough, adding flavor and sometimes color to the finished loaf. Fruit juices may contain sugar (see above).

Gluten-free flours

Gluten-free flours should not comprise more than 25% of the total weight of the flour so as not to unduly weaken the gluten web. Small rolls can include up to 50% gluten-free flour. Use high-protein wheat flour to compensate. You can also add 1 teaspoon pure wheat gluten to a dough per cup of non-wheat flour to compensate.

Mashed potatoes and winter squash

Add mashed potatoes (including yams or sweet potatoes), potato boiling water, winter squash or potato flour to bread dough for added moisture and a soft, fluffy texture. For example, King Arthur Flour's "Holy Grail" whole wheat sandwich bread includes 3 tablespoons potato flour. Potato and squash bread is delicious with fresh herbs like rosemary, lavender, oregano and thyme.

Whole grains and seeds

[Soakers: Whole or cracked grains and seeds added to bread dough. This is a different meaning of the word than Peter Reinhart's soakers made with flour and water described in chapter 7]

Whole and cracked grains and seeds add a delightful crunch and extra nutrition and flavor to bread. Soak grains and seeds before adding them to dough so as not to alter the hydration balance. The ratio of grain to soaking water should be 1:1 by volume. Cracked grains only need an hour of soaking in hot tap water. Pour boiling water over longer-cooking grains for instant presoaking of quick-cooking grains (cool before adding to starter). Alternatively, sprout whole grains until the "tails" just begin to show (see "Make your own diastatic malt" in chapter 7 for directions). Sprouted wheat, barley and rye have a strong malt flavor. Optionally, add 1 teaspoon vital wheat gluten to the dough per cup of grains to create a stronger gluten web.

Fruits and vegetables

For a 1½–2 pound loaf of bread, add up to ¾ cup dried vegetables, fruit or nuts or 1½ cups fresh vegetables or fruit. Dried versions can be soaked like cracked grains before adding to the dough. On the other hand, if you are adding moist vegetables or fruit like fresh onions or apples, you will need to reduce the added liquid by 1 or 2 tablespoons to maintain the hydration level. Raisin tip: use unsoaked raisins to prevent the crumb from darkening; to maintain proper dough hydration, add a little extra water to the dough itself — the raisins will absorb the extra water.

Herbs and spices

For a 1½–2 pound loaf of bread, add up to ½ cup fresh herbs (1–3 tablespoons for intensely flavored herbs like rosemary) or up to 1 tablespoon of dried flaked herbs or whole or ground spices.

Toppings

Salt, sugar, herbs, spices, chopped or slivered nuts and seeds can be spread or sprinkled on top of bread dough, as is commonly done with Italian focaccia. Good sprinkling spices include minced dried onion, whole nigella seeds, fresh rosemary, slivered almonds, and poppy and sesame seeds. Press the salt or spices into the dough before its last rising or apply a glaze of cornstarch and water to act as glue for the seeds.

Be creative

Any type of sourdough bread, except for very thin flatbreads like sourdough tortillas and pita pockets, go great with additional ingredients and flavorings such as whole or cracked grains, non-wheat flours, nuts and seeds, dried fruit and vegetables, herbs and spices. Experiment! I like to be spontaneous and make things up off the top of my head. For example, "tabbouli bread" could contain coarse bulgur, dried tomatoes, fresh or dried parsley, chives and spearmint, and lemon zest or chopped fresh sorrel. Hummus bread might be made with garbanzo grits or mashed, cooked garbanzos, sunflower seed butter, garlic, parsley and lemon peel. Chile corn bread could include dried polenta, roasted green chiles, garlic and ground coriander and fresh cilantro. A recipe for caraway rye could include cracked rye, sunflower and flax seeds and whole caraway seeds. Apple bread would taste great with fresh or dried apple chunks, fresh or boiled cider, and coriander or tropical spices like cinnamon and nutmeg. Add chopped kalamata olives and fresh minced rosemary and garlic to make olive rosemary bread.

Glazes

Glazes can be applied before or after baking. Brush on glazes with a pastry brush. Also see the sweet dough glazes below.

❖ **Crisp crust:** Spray loaf with water before baking for an artisan bread crust.

❖ **Shiny hard crust:** In a small saucepan, whisk ½ cup cold water and 1 teaspoon cornstarch. Heat glaze while whisking until it thickens and becomes translucent. Cool. Brush on bread before baking. Sprinkle seeds if desired — the wash will glue the seeds to the loaf. You can also brush on more glaze immediately after the loaf is taken out of the oven.

❖ **Crisp sweet shiny crust:** Brush baked loaves with a solution of 1 tablespoon each sugar and water.

❖ **Soft brown velvety crust:** Brush on some melted Earth Balance™ (or butter or ghee) before baking.

❖ **Egg- and dairy-free wash:** Brush loaves with warm almond or soy milk before baking. The protein makes a golden crust. Low-protein milks like rice milk will not have the same effect.

❧ 100% whole wheat loaf ❧

Baker's formula

Flour	100%
Water	73%
Salt	2 %
Sweetener	8%
Starch	2%
Flax	4.5%
Total	*189.5%*

To make bread containing unbleached flour, lower the hydration level as needed to maintain the dough consistency (100% white bread needs roughly 10% less water).

This bread works well with whole wheat or whole spelt. It has a 73% hydration, which does not include the agave nectar or honey or the ground flax and potato starch. In this version, ⅜ of the flour is Kamut® for a nutty flavor. Substitute whole wheat or spelt for the Kamut® to make the bread rise higher. To make Russian buckwheat rolls, substitute buckwheat flour for 50% of the whole wheat/kamut flour. Follow the directions for making dinner rolls in chapter 10.

Dough

Ingredient	U.S. Weight	U.S. Volume	Metric
Culture	20 oz	1⅞ cups	567
Whole wheat flour	2 oz	½ cup	56 g
Kamut® flour	4.4 oz	rounded cup	124 g
Water	2 oz	¼ cup	56 g
Salt	0.35 oz	1¾ teaspoons	10 g
Agave nectar/honey	1.3 oz	2 tablespoons	37 g
Potato starch	0.35 oz	1 tablespoon	10 g
Ground flax	0.75 oz	¼ cup	21 g

1. Activate the culture. After 8 oz is returned to the storage jar, there will be 20 oz left for use in the formula.
2. Weigh kamut, water, salt, sweetener, potato starch and flax directly into mixing bowl. Separately weigh out whole wheat flour in a separate bowl. Mix dough until it is too thick to stir.
5. Flour kneading surface with whole wheat or spelt flour. Turn the dough out onto kneading surface and knead rest of flour into the dough, about 10 minutes or until smooth and elastic. Lightly shape into ball.
7. Oil a medium loaf pan and dust with semolina. Stretch dough, place in pan and flatten with hands. Moisten surface with water if you live in a dry climate. Lightly oil surface and cover.
8. Proof until doubled.
9. Preheat oven to 375°F (191°C). Bake about 40 minutes or until lightly browned.

❧ Dan's sandwich bread ❧ with cracked grains

This is my husband's favorite pan bread. It makes one large 2 2/3 lb loaf. I bake it in an extra-large loaf pan that is 4" high x 4 ½" wide x 9 ½" long. The large, square slices are perfect for hearty veggie burgers, cinnamon toast, and PB&J. I use all-purpose flour to produce a lighter, higher-rising bread. The hydration level is deceptively high because it includes the water used to soak the cracked grains.

Baker's formula

Flour	100%
Water	87%
Salt	2.4%
Malt	0.5%
Grains	19.5%
Flax	3.7%
Caraway	1.2%
Total	*214.3%*

Dough

Ingredient	U.S. Weight	U.S. Volume	Metric
Culture	20 oz	1⅞ cups	567 g
Flour	10.5 oz	2 ⅝ cups	298 g
Water	2.5 oz	4½ tablespoons	142 g
Salt	0.5 oz	1½ teaspoons	14 g
Diastatic malt sugar	0.1 oz	1 teaspoon	3 g
Cracked grain	4 oz	⅔ cup	113 g
Ground flax	¾ oz	¼ cup	21 g
Caraway seeds (optional)	¼ oz	2 tablespoons	7 g

If you want to use whole wheat flour, add more water to maintain proper dough consistency. One hundred percent whole wheat dough will require roughly 10% more water.

1. Activate the culture. After 8 oz is returned to the storage jar, there will be 20 oz left for use in the formula.
2. Soak the cracked grain in 2 ½ oz (⅔ cup) water for one hour (if you forget, bring the water to a boil, stir in the grains to expand them, then cool the mash on a plate).
3. Weigh water, salt, malt, soaked grains, flax and caraway seeds directly into mixing bowl. Weigh flour in a separate bowl.
4. Mix in the flour ½ cup at a time until dough is too stiff to stir. Dust the kneading surface. Turn the dough out onto the kneading surface and knead the rest of the flour into the dough, about 10 minutes or until smooth and elastic. Lightly shape into ball.
7. Oil a large loaf pan and dust with semolina. Stretch dough, place in pan and flatten with hands. Moisten surface with water if you live in a dry climate. Oil top lightly and cover.
8. Proof until doubled.
9. Preheat oven to 375°F (191°C). Bake about 45 minutes or until lightly browned.

❧ Savory sourdough crackers ❧

<table>
<tr><td colspan="2">Baker's formula</td></tr>
<tr><td>Flour</td><td>100%</td></tr>
<tr><td>Water</td><td>50%</td></tr>
<tr><td>Oil</td><td>12.5%</td></tr>
<tr><td>Salt</td><td>1.8%</td></tr>
<tr><td>Total</td><td>164.3%</td></tr>
</table>

It is ridiculously easy to make your own crackers. Moreover, crackers can be made with a high percentage of low gluten or gluten-free flours. In this version I've mixed Kamut® and garbanzo flour with whole wheat bread flour for a nutty, savory flavor. Other good flours include spelt, durum (for extra crunch) and rye. I don't like to bake too many trays of crackers at once, so I've used just 6 oz active starter here. Because you can't make just 6 oz of active starter, I make crackers when I am making something else. Feed the starter an extra 3 oz flour and 3 oz water at some point during the activation process. The crackers will fill two large baking trays. Add garlic or onion powder to the dough, or top with kosher salt, poppy, sesame or caraway seeds as desired. If you live in a humid climate, you may need to dry the baked crackers in a low-temperature oven or electric food drier before storing.

Dough

Ingredient	U.S. Weight	U.S. Volume	Metric
Culture	6 oz	Scant ⅔ cup	168 g
Water	3 oz	⅜ cup	84 g
Salt	0.15 oz	½ teaspoon	4 g
Canola or olive oil	1 oz	3 tablespoons	28 g
Whole wheat flour	3 oz	¾ cup	84 g
Kamut® flour	2.5 oz	Scant ⅔ cup	70 g
Garbanzo flour	2.5 oz	Scant ⅔ cup	70 g

1. Weigh out 6 oz active culture for the crackers.
2. Weigh the water, salt, oil, Kamut® and garbanzo flours directly into the mixing bowl containing the culture. Weigh the whole wheat flour in a separate bowl.
3. Use some of the whole wheat flour to dust the kneading board. Turn the dough out onto the board. Knead in most of the rest of the flour until the dough becomes a smooth, stiff ball. Place the dough on a dusting of the remaining flour for the bench rest. If you live in an arid climate, moisten the outside of the dough. Cover. Bench rest at least 20 minutes. If you like thin, crisp crackers, you can roll them out after 20 minutes. For lighter, puffier crackers, allow the dough to rise up to double its initial volume.
4. Preheat oven to 425°F (218°C).

5. Use a bench knife to divide dough into four parts. Dust kneading board with additional flour. Use a rolling pin to roll out each piece of dough to less than ⅛" thick. Sprinkle on optional toppings and lightly press into dough. Use a fork to dock surface. If you skip this step, the crackers will puff like pita bread.

6. Use a knife or fluted pastry cutter to cut the sheet into crackers that are 1–3" wide. Place crackers on an oiled or parchment-lined baking sheet. Roll out a second piece of dough to fill the rest of the baking sheet.

5. Bake the crackers for 7–8 minutes, until the edges begin to brown— crackers can burn very quickly!

6. Roll out and bake second sheet.

7. Cool crackers on a wire rack. Store in an airtight container.

❧ Sweet dough ❧

This is a moderately-rich egg- and dairy-free sweet dough that can be used to make sweet rolls, Danishes, or sweet breads like German stolen . I use 100% all-purpose flour. Feel free to substitute liquid sweeteners like maple syrup or agave nectar in place of the sugar. Count liquid sweeteners as part of the water content.

Dough

Ingredient	U.S. Weight	U.S. Volume	Metric
Culture	20 ounces	1⅞ cups	567 g
Flour	9 oz	2¼ cups	252 g
Water or milk	1.5 oz	3 tablespoons	42 g
Salt	0.3 oz	1½ teaspoons	8 g
Cane sugar	2.7 oz	⅓ cup	76 g
Earth Balance™	2½ oz	⅓ cup	70 g

Baker's formula	
Flour	100%
Water	60.5%
Salt	1.6%
Sugar	16.9%
Fat	15.6%
Total	*194.8%*

If you want to use whole wheat flour, add more water to maintain proper dough consistency. One hundred percent whole wheat dough will require roughly 10% more water.

1. Activate the culture. After 8 oz is returned to the storage jar, there will be 20 oz left for use in the formula.

2. Weigh each ingredient into mixing bowl. Melt Earth Balance™ and cool until lukewarm. Stir in about 6 oz flour, until dough is shaggy. Sprinkle some of the remaining flour on kneading surface. Turn out dough onto floured surface. Knead about 10 minutes, gradually adding more flour as needed, until dough forms a sticky elastic ball. Cover and bench rest 30 minutes.

3. Shape dough as desired (see next page for shaping options).

Roll up each dough section the long way. Slice each log into five spirals. Arrange in a 3 x 5 pattern in a greased 9" x 13" baking dish.

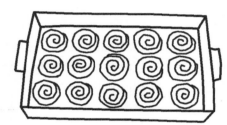

You can turn this bread into a savory dinner loaf by leaving out the cinnamon and sugar and adding other herbs and spices such as sautéed onions and rubbed sage.

Sweet rolls

You'll need additional flour and melted Earth Balance™ for rolling out the dough and basting the sweet rolls in the pan.

1. After bulk fermentation, use a bench knife to divide dough into three pieces. Bench rest for 10 minutes to relax the gluten.
2. Keep pieces covered as each section is rolled out. Roll out each section on a generously floured cutting board until it is about 9" x 12". Sprinkle or spread toppings as desired (I like basting the dough with melted Earth Balance™ and sprinkling the surface with sugar, cinnamon, soy imlk powder and pecans).
3. Roll up each dough section the long way. Slice each log into five spirals. Place rolls upright in a 3 x 5 pattern in a greased 9" x 13" baking dish or arrange in a round pan. If you live in a dry climate, mist the surface with water.
4. Baste rolls with Earth Balance™, cover, and proof until doubled.
5. Bake at 350°F (177°C) until lightly browned, about 30 minutes. Right after you remove the pan from the oven baste rolls with a glaze if desired (see below) or cool rolls and drizzle on a powdered sugar glaze.

Swirled cinnamon pecan bread

In this version, the dough is rolled out and sprinkled with a cinnamon sugar mixture, then rolled up like a giant sweet roll and baked in a loaf pan. Try other nuts and dried fruits in place of the pecans. Underproofing will cause a large hole to form in the center of the swirl due to over-exuberant oven spring.

1. After bench rest, roll out dough on floured surface into a thick rectangular slab. Spread room temperature Earth Balance™. Sprinkle with sugar, cinnamon, and chopped pecans. Roll dough into loaf, being careful to press out the air.
2. Place loaf in greased and semolina-dusted loaf pan. If you live in a dry climate, mist the surface with water. Oil top with canola oil or melted Earth Balance™. Cover and proof until doubled.
3. Bake at 350°F (177°C) about 45 minutes or until crust is lightly browned.
4. Remove loaf from pan and place on wire rack to cool. If desired, baste crust with melted Earth Balance™ or another glaze.

Braided holiday bread

This bread is loosely inspired by Jewish challah (HALL-uh), traditionally made with lots of egg yolks. Challah is often sprinkled with poppy or sesame seeds. Brush on a cornstarch wash to help the seeds to stick to the surface and produce a brown, shiny crust. You'll need additional flour and melted Earth Balance™ for rolling out the dough and basting the loaf.

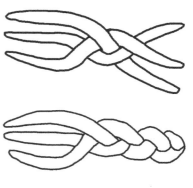

Begin braiding the holiday bread in the middle (top). To make a ring (bottom), curve the dough in a circle and attach the two ends of dough to each other with a little pressure.

1. To add a yellow color to the dough, heat the water or milk to near boiling and sprinkle in a pinch of ground saffron. Allow saffron to soak and release its color into liquid. Allow water to cool down to lukewarm before mixing dough.

2. After bench rest, divide dough into three sections. On a generously floured surface, roll each section into a thick 12–14" rope, as if rolling a clay coil. Taper the ends.

3. To braid ropes together, lay them next to each other on a parchment-lined or greased peel or baking sheet. Begin braid in middle as shown in picture and braid outward. Tuck the ends underneath the dough. You can also shape the braid into a circle. Baste dough with melted Earth Balance™ or a cornstarch wash (p. 107). Sprinkle on seeds if desired. Cover and let rise until doubled.

4. Preheat oven to 350°F (177°C). Slide loaf off peel onto baking stone or place baking tray in oven. Bake about 30 minutes, until lightly browned. If loaf was basted with Earth Balance™, rather than sprinkled with seeds, you can baste crust with more melted Earth Balance™ or another glaze after you take it out of the oven.

5. Cool loaf on a wire rack before storing.

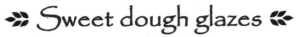

Sweet dough glazes

Baste or drizzle after baking. If the bread is still hot, the glaze will soak into the crust. If you wait until the bread is cool, the glaze will be more like icing:

❖ **Soft sticky crust:** Before or after baking, brush on warmed agave nectar, maple syrup, apricot jam or honey. Brushing the glaze before baking darkens the crust.

❖ **Powdered sugar glaze:** Mix ⅓ cup powdered or confectioner's sugar with ½ tablespoon lemon juice or milk. Wait until bread is cool before drizzling.

❖ **Powdered soy milk glaze:** Mix ½ cup Better Than Milk™ powder (any flavor) with ¼ cup warmed agave nectar, maple syrup or honey. Wait until bread is cool before drizzling.

❖ **Flavored glazes:** Add ¼ teaspoon flavor extract to one of the above glazes.

❖ **Cinnamon sugar topping:** Brush baked bread with 2 tablespoons melted Earth Balance™, then sprinkle with a cinnamon-sugar mixture.

No-knead batter bread

This bread is similar to quickbread, with a super-moist crumb, but a chewier texture and sourdough flavor. Add other ingredients like dried fruit, herbs and spices as desired. I like using this formula to make cinnamon raisin bread with 1 tablespoon cinnamon and 1 cup raisins. Proof and bake the bread in a glass, ceramic or stainless steel loaf pan. Never use an aluminum pan; the wet, acidic batter will etch visible markings into the surface.

Baker's formula

Flour	100%
Liquid	78%
Salt	1.8%
Sugar	5.7%
Fat	5.7%
Total	191.2%

Dough

Ingredient	U.S. Weight	U.S. Volume	Metric
Culture	20 ounces	1⅞ cups	567 g
Milk	6 oz	¾ cup	168 g
Canola oil or Earth Balance™	0.8 oz	2 tablespoons	22 g
Cane sugar	0.8 oz	2 tablespoons	22 g
Salt	¼ oz	1½ teaspoons	8 g
Whole wheat flour	4 oz	1 cup	112 g

1. Activate culture. After 8 oz is returned to storage jar, there will be 20 oz left for use in formula.
2. Melt Earth Balance™ (if using). Add milk to Earth Balance™ to cool it down. If the milk is cold, warm it to luke-warm. Stir liquid into culture.
3. Weigh out sugar and salt into the batter and mix to combine.
2. Weigh out flour into mixing bowl and mix to remove most of the lumps.
3. Pour batter into loaf pan or bowl that has been oiled and sprinkled with semolina or cornmeal. Cover and proof until doubled in bulk.
4. Preheat oven to 350°F (177°C). Bake about 45 minutes or until lightly browned.
6. Turn loaf upside down onto a cooling rack.

Bread oven from the Roman city of Pompeii. The city was buried in ashes from an eruption of Mount Vesuvius in 79 AD. The lower opening is the space where the wood was burned. The upper space is where the bread was baked. See a carbonized loaf of spelt bread baked in one of the city's bak-eries on p. 14.

12
Stovetop breads

"A crust eaten in peace is better than a banquet partaken in anxiety."

— Aesop

The basics: In pre-fossil fuel eras, wood was often scarce, especially in the Old World. Traditional bread ovens were communal. Individual households often made do with small cooking fires. The result was a delicious array of skillet breads — flatbreads, pancakes, crêpes, English muffins, and steamed dumplings. To cook skillet breads, preheat non-stick or cast iron skillet on medium for 10–15 minutes. You want the metal fully heated through. Do not turn the temperature up too high; that will burn the bread. If the pan is not non-stick, lightly grease with Earth Balance™ or canola oil.

❧ Pancakes, crêpes & waffles ☙

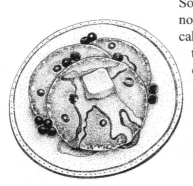

Sourdough pancakes, crêpes and waffles have a depth of flavor not found in quickbread versions. A plain flour and water pancake batter with a pinch of salt tastes great all by itself. If you thin the batter to the consistency of thick cream, you have crêpes (use a whisk to remove lumps).

❖ My favorite pancake/crêpe recipe is to take some active starter, add a tablespoon or two of melted Earth Balance™, a tablespoon or two of sugar or liquid sweetener, a splash of milk, and enough additional flour to maintain my desired batter consistency. I like ground flax seeds too. I fry pancakes and crêpes in melted Earth Balance™. Look up your own favorite pancake recipe and add those ingredients to active starter to create your own sourdough version.

❖ Pancakes and crêpes work well with gluten-free flours. Use buckwheat to make hearty buckwheat flapjacks or dainty Russian blini (small-diameter crêpes). Add tef flour to the batter to make Ethiopian injera. Use blue cornmeal for a beautiful purple color. You'll find another recipe for 100% gluten-free Ethiopian injera in chapter 15.

❖ Waffle batter contains more fat and sugar, which create a crispier texture and increased caramelization of the surface. The three-dimensional honeycomb texture of waffles increases the crispness too. Waffle irons come in electric and stovetop versions. Follow the directions for your iron.

❧ Sourdough wraps ❧

Arabic khubz saj *(yeasted thin bread) is similar to Spanish wheat tortillas, but puffier like Indian naan. I use sourdough wraps for bean burritos, scrambled tofu and much more. The dough can be kept covered in a refrigerator and rolled out as needed for several days. Allow refrigerated dough to warm up at room temperature about one hour to relax the gluten before rolling out the wraps.*

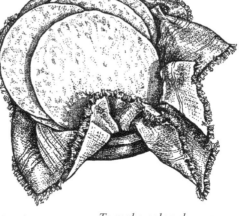

1. Make basic artisan dough as described in chapter 10. Preheat griddle to medium/medium-high heat, until a drop of water dances on the surface. Prepare a towel or reclosable plastic bag for storing wraps until serving time.

2. After bench rest, gently flatten dough on floured surface. Use bench knife or serrated knife to slice dough into pieces. Keep dough lumps covered as you roll out each wrap. Dust a little flour on dough board. Flatten a piece of dough with your palm and use rolling pin to roll dough out to ⅛" thick or less. Begin at center and roll out toward edges, rotating 90° between rolls to keep shape even.

3. If you are not using a non-stick griddle, lightly oil it. Cook first side 2–3 minutes, or until brown spots appear. Flip over wrap and cook another 2–3 minutes. The bread will puff up a little.

4. To keep finished breads warm and pliable until you are ready to serve, stack them in a reclosable plastic bag and fold a towel on top (or wrap breads in a couple of towels).

To make colored wraps, add a tablespoon of spinach powder, beet powder, tomato powder or tomato paste or a pinch of saffron soaked in hot water for 10 minutes.

❧ Flaky herbed flatbread ❧

This is one of the few breads in this book in which unbleached flour works better than whole wheat. Whole wheat dough doesn't stretch as well as dough made from unbleached flour, and you don't want the herbs and spices to tear the dough. Choose fresh herbs and spices that go with the rest of the meal. I like to use ground, toasted cumin and black pepper and chopped fresh cilantro. I also like to sprinkle on ground sumac for a tangy Middle Eastern flavor.

1. Make basic artisan dough in chapter 10 using unbleached flour. Preheat griddle to medium/medium-high heat, until a drop of water dances on the surface. Prepare towel or reclosable plastic bag for storing wraps until serving time.
2. After bench rest, gently flatten dough on floured surface. Use bench knife or serrated knife to slice dough into small egg-sized pieces. Keep dough lumps covered as you roll out wraps.
3. Dust a little flour on dough board. Roll out each piece of dough to ⅛" thick, as if making a sourdough wrap. Brush the surface with melted Earth Balance™ and sprinkle evenly with salt, herbs and spices.
4. Roll circle of dough into a rope. Curve rope into a spiral, pressing the end into rest of dough. Flatten spiral with your hand, then use a rolling pin to roll dough into a circle less than ¼" thick.
5. If you are not using a non-stick griddle, lightly oil griddle. Cook first side 2–3 minutes, or until brown spots begin to appear. Flip over and bake second side.
6. To keep finished breads warm and pliable until you are ready to serve, stack them in a 10" diameter reclosable plastic bag and fold a towel on top (or skip bag and wrap breads in a couple of towels).

❧ English muffins ❧

You haven't tasted an English muffins until you've tried the sourdough version. Use basic artisan dough as is or use 2 tablespoons melted Earth Balance™ or canola oil and milk in place of water. After bulk fermentation and bench rest, roll out sections of dough to ½" thick (dough can also be wrapped and stored in a refrigerator for a day or two before rolling out). Cut out muffins with round 3–4" diameter biscuit cutter. Place muffins on flour- or semolina-dusted board or oiled baking tray. Re-knead scraps and cut more muffins. You'll end up with about 16 muffins. Alternatively, cut 16 square muffins with a bench knife. Spray or pat with water if you live in a dry climate. Cover and proof until doubled. Fry muffins on an oiled medium-hot griddle (canola works well) like pancakes for several minutes on each side until lightly browned. Don't make griddle too hot or crusts will burn before insides are fully cooked. Cool on wire rack. To serve, split muffins open lengthwise.

❧ Steamed stew dumplings ❧

Make English muffin formula and proof until doubled (add herbs to dough if desired). Gently place dough rounds in a bubbling pot of stew. Close lid and steam 10 minutes or until done.

13
Specialty breads

"Bread has a history of both sustaining great empires and inciting revolution."
— Emily Beuhler, *Bread Science*

The basics: This is a catch-all chapter for wheat breads that don't fit into the previous categories. You'll learn how to grill flatbreads, poach bagels and soft pretzels before baking, fry doughnuts, and make sourdough quickbreads that include baking soda or baking powder.

≫ Grilled flatbread ≪

Heat an indoor stovetop grill or uncovered outdoor grill (wood, charcoal or gas). Grilled sourdough flatbread has a wonderful puffy quality and develops grill marks. The basic artisan bread formula in chapter 10 works well. Thinner flatbreads (⅛–¼" thick) cook in about the same time as in a skillet. Flip over to brown the second side. For thicker (½") flatbreads, make several slashes across the top to allow the bread to fully cook in the center. Be careful not to let the flames burn the bread.

❧ 100% whole wheat bagels ❧

Bagels and related breads like soft pretzels require pre-boiling (actually, poaching) in an alkaline solution before baking for a shiny, chewy crust. The dough is very dry so that it will not fall apart when poached. The poaching allows wheat starch on the dough surface to gelatinize. When the dough is baked, the gelatinized starch forms a crisp, chewy, dark crust.

Baker's formula	
Flour	100%
Water	56%
Salt	1.8%
Malt	7%
Total	*164.8%*

❖ Jewish bagels are traditionally made from unbleached high-gluten flour and sweetened with barley malt syrup. The high gluten flour and dry texture of bagel dough create a super-chewy, fine-textured crumb. Bagels made with 100% whole wheat flour will be somewhat less chewy and more bread-like. If you want to use some or all unbleached flour, I recommend King Arthur Flour's Sir Lancelot Hi-Gluten Flour, the highest gluten flour (14.2% protein) available to home bakers. High gluten flour requires a similar hydration to whole wheat flour.

❖ If desired, substitute rice syrup, agave nectar, maple syrup or honey for the barley malt syrup.

❖ A classic New York bagel is made from 4 oz of dough. My formula begins with 18 oz of active sourdough culture to make a dough that is divided into eight 4 oz bagels. Larger bagels have a doughier texture and smaller bagels a crispier texture. Make your bagels whatever size you prefer.

❖ Bagels have holes to ensure even baking. Some cookbooks tell you to make the holes by poking your finger through a ball of dough. However, holes made using that method tend to shrink. The traditional technique is to make a rope of dough and then attach the two ends together to form a ring.

❖ Traditionally, the poaching solution is made by adding 1 part lye to 64 parts water. Lye (sodium hydroxide or NaOH) is highly corrosive. Before the modern era lye was leached from wood ashes. Working with lye requires rubber gloves and goggles. I use a less dangerous substitute, baking soda, which is also an alkaline substance.

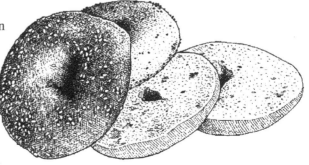

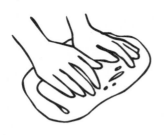

Bagel dough is very stiff and requires a lot of kneading. Take breaks!

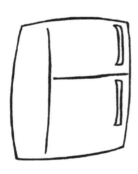

Refrigerating the bagels before poaching is optional. Because retarding the dough is done to develop flavor, its not necessary when using a strongly flavored sourdough starter.

Dough

Ingredient	U.S. Weight	U.S. Volume	Metric
Culture	18 ounces	1⅝ cups	504 g
Flour	11.5 oz	2¼ cups	322 g
Water	1.5 oz	1¼ cups	42 g
Salt	0.3 oz	1½ teaspoons	8 g
Barley malt syrup	1 oz	1½ tablespoons	28 g

1. Activate culture by feeding it three times with 1.8 oz each flour and water. After 8 oz is returned to storage jar, there will be 18 oz left for use in formula.

2. Weigh out water, salt and barley malt directly into bowl. Mix until dough is too thick to stir.

3. Weigh out flour in separate bowl. Dust kneading board with some of the flour and use plastic scraper to turn dough out onto board. Start kneading, adding flour as you go. Because this dough is very dry, you'll have to knead for longer than usual to hydrate all the flour and properly develop the gluten. I like to knead for 5 minute intervals with 5 minutes rests in between. Cover dough during each rest. After about 25 minutes total kneading, the dough will become a smooth elastic ball.

4. Bench rest 30 minutes. Many bagel makers do an overnight fermentation in the refrigerator for extra flavor. If you choose to do this, moisten outside of ball with water, oil surface and wrap loosely with plastic wrap so dough does not burst out of wrap as it rises. Place in produce bin of refrigerator to keep moist.

5. If the dough has been in the refrigerator overnight, remove it and allow it to warm up to room temperature for 30 minutes to an hour. Add 4" water to a stock pot and heat to a boil while rolling out bagels. Preheat oven to 500°F (260°C).

6. Do not flour kneading surface (or else use as little flour as possible). Gently de-gas dough. Use bench knife or serrated knife to divide into 8 pieces weighing about 4 oz each. Roll each piece into ball and set aside. Cover unused dough as you roll out each bagel. Roll each ball into a rope with your hand. Alternatively, roll out entire mass of dough into ½" thick rectangular slab and use bench knife to cut strips ½" wide x 8–10" long.

7. Wrap coils around your knuckles to make a ring. If the two ends are in your palm, you can then roll the ends together briefly on the kneading board to seal together. Bench rest rings for 10 minutes before poaching.

8. Just before you start poaching the dough, add 2 teaspoons baking soda to poaching water. The water will foam and then settle back down. The boil should be low so that the bagels are gently poached. A rapid boil can cause dough to disintegrate. Gently place a couple of bagels in water. They will float within 10 seconds. Poach 45 seconds then turn them over and poach second sides another 45 seconds. Poached bagels will look wrinkly.

Dumpling strainer.

9. Use Chinese dumpling strainer (available at Asian markets and kitchen stores) or large slotted spoon to remove bagels from water. Place on large parchment-lined or greased baking tray. Poach remaining bagels. If desired, brush tops with cornstarch glaze (chapter 11) and sprinkle with poppy or sesame seeds.

10. Slide tray into oven. Pour some water into your cast iron frying pan to create steam just as you would for artisan breads (p. 87). Close oven door, turn down heat to 450°F (232°C) and bake 15 minutes. Remove tray, turn over bagels and bake another 15 minutes, until crusts are golden brown. Cool on wire rack until cool enough to handle (if you're going to eat them right away) or until they reach room temperature (if they will be stored).

❧ Soft pretzels ❦

Woodcuts of historical pretzel shapes.

Make bagel dough. Follow the basic bagel process. Divide dough into 8–12 pieces. Roll out each piece in a thin rope less than ½" thick. Taper the ends. Loop ropes into pretzel shapes as desired (use your creativity) and gently press dough pieces together where they touch. Poach pretzels less than 30 seconds a side and arrange on parchment lined or greased baking tray. Baste with cornstarch glaze and sprinkle with coarse kosher salt, poppy seeds or sesame seeds. Bake at 450°F (232°C) 12–15 minutes, until deep golden brown. Alternatively, leave off the cornstarch glaze and toppings and brush with melted Earth Balance™ as soon as the pretzels come out of the oven, then dust with cinnamon sugar. Or add rye flour and caraway seeds to the dough for a central European flavor.

❧ Yeast doughnuts ❧

I use my basic sweet dough formula to make doughnuts. You can also use lean artisan dough.

❖ The simplest doughnut shape is a blobby ball, otherwise known as a "doughnut hole."

❖ To make doughnuts with holes, roll the dough out to about ⅜" thick and cut with a doughnut cutter or improvise by using your finger to poke a hole through each doughnut. The hole in the dough allows heat to flow around the dough for even cooking.

Doughnut holes (top) and doughnuts with holes.

❖ Choose a neutral-flavored oil with a high smoke point, such as canola, soy or refined coconut oil. Pour several inches of oil into a heavy-bottomed pot. I prefer to heat up the oil half-way on medium-low for 20–30 minutes and then turn the temperature up to frying temperature (375°F/191°C)) just before the dough is ready to fry. Use a candy thermometer (available at supermarkets) to measure temperature. If the temperature is too low it will take a long time to cook the dough, causing it to dry out too much. Higher temperatures will cause the dough to brown too much before the inside is fully cooked.

❖ After the bulk fermentation, roll or shape the dough into your preferred shapes. Keep the unused dough covered as you fry. Don't crowd the pot. Cook each side a couple of minutes, until lightly browned. Use a slotted spoon or Chinese dumpling strainer to remove the doughnuts. Drain on a towel-lined plate.

❖ Homemade doughnuts are absolutely delicious as is. For even greater decadence, roll in powdered sugar, dip in melted chocolate or use the doughnut glaze recipe below.

❧ Doughnut glaze ❧

Use a whisk to mix 2 cups confectioners' sugar with ½ cup hot water. While the doughnuts are still hot, use tongs to dip them in the glaze. Place on waxed paper or parchment paper to dry.

❧ Sopapillas ❧

Sopapillas (soap-uh-PEE-yuhs) are the New Mexican answer to doughnuts. The little deep fried pillows means "fried dough sweetened with honey" in Spanish. While some sopapilla recipes use sweet dough, I prefer using lean artisan dough. Simply roll the dough out to ⅛" thick and slice in small triangles 3–6 inches across, then place in fryer. Sopapillas are traditionally eaten drizzled with honey and butter (for a vegan alternative, agave nectar, maple syrup and Earth Balance™ are absolutely delicious). Bite off one corner and pour the liquid sweetener or a pat of Earth Balance™ inside the sopapilla. If you fry larger, thicker rounds of dough, you have Native American frybread. Navajo tacos use a large round of frybread as a base for tostada toppings like refried beans, tomatoes and lettuce.

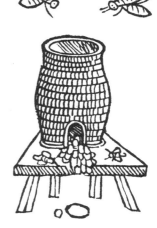

Medieval woodcut of a beehive.

❧ Sourdough quickbreads ❧

You can substitute active sourdough starter in any quickbread, muffin, baking soda biscuit, biscuit, dumpling, or cake recipe leavened with either baking soda or baking powder. Sourdough "quickbreads" have the flavor of sourdough but the fluffy, unkneaded texture of quickbread.

❖ To convert a recipe, tally up the flours and liquids to determine the hydration percentage. Make sure the final hydration level is the same as in the original recipe. Treat the batter like sourdough batter bread (chapter 11); avoid too much mixing or kneading so as not to overdevelop the gluten (you want the unorganized gluten links of a quickbread or cake).

❖ When the batter is fully proofed, gently mix in the chemical leavener and bake as directed in the original recipe. For recipes using baking soda, leave out the acidic ingredient (usually vinegar, lemon juice or soured milk). The sourdough starter provides enough acid to react with the baking soda to create bubbles of carbon dioxide. Because baking soda neutralizes acid, it removes the sour flavor, but leaves a yeasty aroma and the other flavor molecules produced by the lactobacteria. Baking powder contains its own acid and will not affect the sourdough flavor as much.

14
Rye breads

"Whose bread I eat: his song I sing."
— German proverb

The basics: Rye bread is a traditional staple of northern European countries where the climate is too cold or damp for cultivating wheat. High-percentage rye doughs require special handling. If you just want to add some rye flavor to bread but want the ease of making wheat bread, you can substitute up to 20% of the wheat flour with rye flour with no major changes to your bread making method.

Is it really rye?

Caraway seeds, the scent that people most often associate with rye bread.

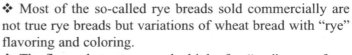

❖ Most of the so-called rye breads sold commercially are not true rye breads but variations of wheat bread with "rye" flavoring and coloring.

❖ The flavor that many people think of as "rye" comes from caraway seeds. Open up a jar of caraway seeds and take a sniff. If this is the case with you, you may be happy adding whole, toasted or ground caraway seeds to wheat bread.

❖ Many traditional peasant rye breads were actually a mix of wheat and rye known as "maslin" that was grown together in the same field. In a cool, wet year the rye would thrive. In a hot, dry year the wheat would thrive. The grains were harvested and ground together.

❖ Jewish-style rye breads are fairly low in rye flour. Their special flavor and texture comes from a type of refined wheat flour called first clear flour, a high-protein and high-ash (mineral) flour which provides a lot of flavor and a distinctive chewy texture. Of course, caraway flavor is intrinsic to Jewish rye breads, too.

❖ While whole rye bread has a natural gray-brown color, the dark brown color of many commercial "rye" breads actually comes from caramelized sugar. Some recipes also contain other dark ingredients like cocoa powder or molasses, ingredients that would not have been available to the average European peasant.

❖ One hypothesis I have is that dark rye peasant breads contained acorn flour. Acorns were a common food of the poor for thousands of years. Acorn flour produces a very dark brown color and adds a nice tea-like flavor from tannins, like black tea. Commercial acorn flour is available from Korean groceries, where it is usually labeled "acorn starch." As with other gluten-free flours, you don't want to add more than 25% to a wheat or rye dough.

❖ Good spices for adding to rye breads (besides caraway) include anise, cardamom, coriander, dill, nigella and orange zest. Rye bread goes well served with strongly flavored foods like mustard, onions, sauerkraut and dill pickles.

Real rye bread *is* sourdough bread

Sourdough starters are the ideal way to make rye bread containing more than 20% rye. In fact, doughs composed mostly of rye must be made with sourdough. That is because the starches that hold together rye bread are stabilized by an acidic pH below 4.5 (sourdough starters have a natural pH of 4–4.5—p. 19). Alkaline baker's yeast doughs cause rye starches to disintegrate into a gummy mass and produce a bland bread flavor.

❖ To make a 100% rye sourdough culture, you can catch your own wild yeast and bacteria in rye flour, following the directions in chapter 3.

❖ Only one company, GEM Cultures, sells an authentic 100% rye starter (appendix A).

❖ You can also take any wheat-based sourdough starter and feed it rye flour to convert it into a rye starter. The Austria culture from Sourdoughs International is especially compatible with doughs containing up to 100% rye.

[Sauerteig: A traditional German rye sourdough starter]

The types of rye flour

Rye flour comes in a range of forms related to the extraction (refining) level. Rye flour is refined and oxidized in a similar manner to wheat flour. Refer to chapter 5 for more detailed information on the refining and oxidation of flour.

❖ **White rye:** center of endosperm only, artificially bleached
❖ **Medium rye:** entire endosperm (first clear flour used for Jewish rye bread is in this category)
❖ **Dark rye:** contains the bran, but not the germ
❖ **Pumpernickel:** coarsely-ground whole kernel rye, including the bran and germ

Handle with care

Although rye contains gluten, that gluten is composed solely of gliadin—the extensible protein. It has no glutenin proteins to form a tight gluten web. Instead, rye doughs are held together solely by gummy starches known as pentosans. In addition, rye starch granules are larger than wheat starch granules and rye flour contains more amylase enzymes, the flour enzymes that break down starch into sugar, than does wheat flour. During baking, rye starches are very susceptible to attack by the amylase enzymes, too many of which will turn the dough into a sticky, gummy mess.

Due to these characteristics, rye dough is wetter and stickier than wheat dough. Mix gently to hydrate the starch. Never vigorously mix or knead rye dough — overdevelopment creates a sticky, tough dough structure, and there is no gluten web to develop. Gradually work your way up to 100% rye to develop your handling skills.

Rye dough cannot hold its shape. High-percentage rye dough is usually proofed in a baking pan. In addition, slashing is not necessary with high-percentage rye doughs—there is no oven spring, because there is no gluten web to trap the heated air.

Bake rye bread at a moderate temperature (300–400°F/149–204°C). High temperatures lead to more amylase activity, which create a gummy texture.

Cooling & storing rye bread

It is even more important to fully cool rye bread before slicing than to cool wheat bread. As with wheat breads, the crumb structure of cooled rye bread is formed by starch gelatinization. You want to ensure that the gummy pentosans fully gelatinize. Rye bread keeps well for several weeks when wrapped in plastic or several layers of cotton or linen cloth to prevent staling.

Eating rye bread

Rye bread is naturally denser than wheat bread due to the lack of oven spring. Slice rye bread thinly to offset the dense structure. Rye breads are also excellent when toasted (chapter 18).

Make rye pretzels by adding rye flour to the pretzel formula in the previous chapter.

Many traditional central and northern European rye "breads" are crackers designed for long-term storage. See the cracker formula on p. 110.

15
Gluten-free sourdoughs

Yásati: "(it) boils"
— Sanskrit word for yeast

The basics: Gluten-free grains are traditionally used around the world to make sourdough crêpes and dumplings. Ethiopian injera and Indian dosa are easy crêpe recipes for beginners.

Prehistoric fermentations

The world's first leavened "breads" were most likely the result of grain porridge spontaneously fermenting due to the presence of wild yeasts and bacteria. Fermented porridges are found all over the world—in Europe, Asia, the Middle East, Africa and North and South America.

❖ Across much of sub-Saharan Africa, people subsist on sour fermented porridges made from corn, millet or sorghum.

❖ In Central America and the American Southwest, people make a fermented maize dumpling called *pozol* (Aztec *pozolli*, or "foamy") that is wrapped in corn husks and steamed like tamales. In the American Southwest, the Zuni people fermented corn dumpling dough in clay pots set near the hearth.

❖ In Ghana, Africa, people use introduced maize to make a very similar dumpling called kenkey.

❖ In Ethiopia, the tiny cereal grain tef is used to make crêpes called *injera* that are eaten at every meal.

❖ In India, rice and black gram legumes are fermented into *dosa* (crêpes) and *idli* (dumplings).

❧ Ethiopian injera ❧

If you make crêpe batter (with any flour) and allow it to sit longer than 8 hours, it begins to noticeably ferment.

❖ Injera batter is left to ferment for 24–48 hours and becomes increasingly sour in flavor (injera batter is called ersho in Amharic, the language of Ethiopia).

❖ A non-stick pan is recommended. Crêpe pans are nice, but not absolutely necessary.

❖ The spongy crêpes are traditionally made a couple feet in diameter in large skillets over open fires. Stew is ladled on top of the soft, spongy bread and diners break off pieces to scoop up mouthfuls of stew. In a modern American kitchen it's much easier to make smaller crêpes a few inches across.

❖ Tef injera keeps its soft texture for several days if properly wrapped to keep it moist. Injera made from wheat or other flours like millet, sorghum, or barley tends to stale and harden within 24 hours.

❖ Multiply the volume of batter as desired.

1 cup tef, quinoa, amaranth, millet, sorghum, or rice flour
1 cup water
Pinch salt (optional)

1. Whisk flour and water together in bowl. Cover and let sit for at least 4 hours to allow the starches to absorb the water. For good sourdough flavor, let the batter sit 24–48 hours. Whisk a couple of times a day to keep mixture aerated. Alternatively, you can use a few tablespoons of your regular sourdough culture as a starting point to begin the fermentation process.
2. Just before cooking, add a pinch of salt to taste and water as needed to produce batter with the consistency of thick cream.
3. Preheat a crêpe pan or skillet on medium. Make sure metal is fully heated through before cooking. Pour a thin layer of batter in a spiral pattern, beginning at outside edge and moving inward to the center. This ensures that the crêpe will cook evenly. Grip skillet handle and rotate pan to smooth out batter.
4. Cook one crêpe at a time. Pile them on a plate and cover with a second, overturned plate to keep moist while cooking remaining crêpes.

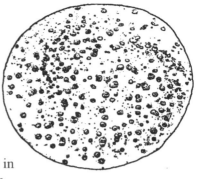

Ethiopian injera and Indian dosa (next page) have a spongy, pliable texture just like wheat crêpes.

[Tef: The world's tiniest grain—$\frac{1}{32}$ of an inch in diameter. One wheat berry weighs as much as 150 grains of tef. "Tef" means "lost" in Amharic, the language of Ethiopia. Because tef grains are so small, the ratio of bran and germ to the starchy endosperm is very high, making the grain highly nutritious. Tef flour is usually ground from brown tef, but there is a white variety you can grind yourself. Tef has a sweet molasses flavor. Tef contains mucilaginous starches that help bind the batter together without gluten. Amaranth and millet have a similar mucilaginous texture and make good substitutes.]

ದೋಸೆ

"Dosa" written in the language of Kannada, spoken in the South Indian state of Karnataka, where the dosa originated.

You can also use a rice-based, gluten-free sourdough starter in place of the soaked rice. Soak and puree the legumes by themselves, then blend with the starter.

❧ Indian dosa ❧

Dosa are very similar to injera. The difference is that they are made from a blended mixture of soaked grains and legumes. Rice is the traditional base, although millet is sometimes used too. Hulled black gram legumes (urad dal), which are white inside, are most commonly used in India to make an ivory-colored crêpe. Using yellow split peas as a substitute creates a beautiful golden color.

½ cup dried urad dal, yellow split peas or split red lentils
1½ cups white or brown long grain rice or pearl millet

1. Combine dal and rice in a stainless steel, glass or ceramic bowl. Cover with 3" cold water. Cover bowl and soak 8–12 hours.
2. Drain soaked grains, reserving 1 cup soaking water. Purée in blender or food processor with the reserved soaking water.
3. Pour batter back into bowl, cover and ferment just like Ethiopian injera batter.
4. Follow injera cooking directions.

❧ Gluten-free loaf bread ❧

Gluten-free grains are combined with gluten-free binders like tapioca starch and xanthan gum to make high rising loaf breads that resemble wheat breads. Cookbooks that specialize in gluten-free breads sometimes include recipes for "sourdough" bread made with baker's yeast. Substitute the real thing instead! Make your own gluten-free starter (chapter 2) or buy the certified gluten-free brown rice starter from GEM Cultures (appendix A). Convert the recipe to sourdough (chapter 6). Maintain the same hydration level of the dough and proceed as directed.

Part IV
Sustainable bread

"Acorns were good till bread was found."
— Francis Bacon

16
Solar bread

"One's own simple bread is much better than someone else's pilaf."
— Azerbaijani proverb

The basics: The most sustainable way to bake bread is with free energy from the sun. A solar cooker collects sunlight and transforms it into heat. It is possible to bake loaf bread, flatbread, pizza, pancakes, crêpes and more in a solar cooker. Solar-baked bread has a soft, fluffy texture and a thin, lightly browned crust.

The sunny side of cooking

At the dawn of the 21st century, the need for sustainable cooking solutions is great because of fossil fuel-caused global warming and climate change, rising energy costs due to the end of cheap oil, fossil fuel pollution, and deforestation (globally, most firewood is cut down for cooking).

❖ Solar cooking is an option across most of the North American continent for at least three seasons of the year.

❖ Depending on the cooker design and weather conditions, solar cooker temperatures range from 180–500°F/82–260°C or higher.

❖ Solar cookers come in a variety of designs suited for every climate, budget, living situation, skill level and cooking need. You can build your own from scraps of cardboard or wood or choose from a variety of commercial models.

The power of light

Solar cookers harness visible sunlight in three ways. Some cookers use just one or two of these techniques. Some use all three:

❖ **A miniature greenhouse effect:** Short-wave visible sunlight enters through clear glass or plastic glazing. The light transforms into longer-wavelength, infrared energy (heat) inside the cooking box. Because it cannot pass back out through the glazing, the temperature rises inside the cooker.

❖ **Sunlight concentration** using reflectors or a foiled cooker interior. The closer to a parabolic shape the reflectors are, the higher the temperature at the point of concentration.

❖ **Insulation** to retain the collected heat.

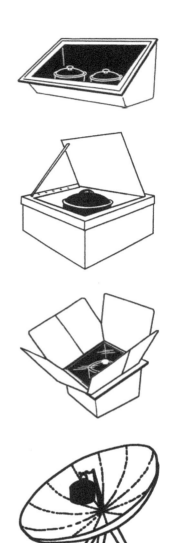

These are the best types of solar cookers for baking bread because they reach the hottest temperatures. Generally speaking, the bigger the cooker, the higher the maximum temperature:

❖ **Single reflector box cooker:** A rectangular box with horizontal glazing. The reflector shines sunlight into the oven chamber. The reflector is propped open with a stick. Single reflector box cookers reach a maximum temperature of 275–300°F/135–149°C.

❖ **Multiple reflector oven:** Four or more reflectors which open up like flower petals to form a crude parabola and slanted glazing. Multiple-reflector ovens reach 250–450°F/121–232°C.

❖ **Parabolic reflector:** Looking like a large satellite dish, parabolic cookers concentrate sunlight onto a single point. They reach 500°F/260°C or higher very quickly and are used just like a stovetop burner for making skillet breads.

Here in sunny Arizona, I solar cook year-round on my townhome balcony in a Global Sun Oven™. My Sun Oven™ has four reflectors that concentrate sunlight in a 14" x 14" oven chamber with a clear glass door. Temperatures generally hover between 325–350°F (163–177°C). The reflectors fold over the glazing for easy storage. I leave the cooker outside and protect it when not in use with a barbecue cover. To learn more about how to choose and operate a solar cooker, see my book *The Sunny Side of Cooking: Solar cooking and other ecologically friendly cooking methods for the 21st century* (2007).

Two simple box cookers (top), a Global Sun Oven™ with four reflectors, and a parabolic reflector.

Black graniteware roasters (top) and cast iron pots, pans, griddles and muffin tins are excellent for baking bread in solar cookers.

The easiest way to bake a loaf of bread in a solar box cooker is to use a round 3-liter graniteware roaster.

Solar bread basics

❖ Baking raw dough requires clear, sunny skies between 10 a.m. and 2 p.m. when sunlight is strongest. 1 lb dough will bake in about one hour in a multiple reflector box cooker. Breads baked in a solar box cooker will lightly brown through the Maillard reaction, but the crust will not caramelize (chapter 9).

❖ Solar cooking requires the use of dark-colored pots and pans. Dark colors absorb sunlight, while light colors reflect light away. The most popular solar cooking pot is a round, covered, 3-liter (10" diameter) black, speckled graniteware roaster available at many supermarkets, camping stores, and online retailers. Keep the lid on while baking.

❖ Cast iron pots and pans are another good option. Preheat cast iron for at least an hour and use like a baking stone (you can't use a real baking stone in a solar cooker; ceramic materials do not heat up properly). Cover pots and pans with a dark lid (I turn my graniteware pot upside down to cover my cast iron tortilla pan).

Freeform artisan bread

Preheat a cast iron tortilla pan or griddle in a box cooker. Slide proofed bread onto griddle. Cover griddle and bake.

Solar loaf bread

A 1–1½ lb loaf of bread fits in a covered 3-liter graniteware roaster. For a rectangular loaf, spray paint the outsides of two loaf pans black, and turn one upside down on top of the other.

Dinner rolls

Solar cookers make especially light, fluffy rolls. For the last proofing, shape 1 lb of dough into 6–12 balls. Lightly oil them and arrange in a 3-liter graniteware roaster. Proof and bake.

Sweet rolls

½ lb of dough makes enough rolls to fit a 3-liter graniteware roaster. 1 lb of dough fills a 9" x 13" baking dish. Cover baking dish with another (dark) overturned baking dish.

Pizza and focaccia

When making pizza, partially bake the crust first, then add the toppings and finish baking. Flatten ½ lb of prepared dough (2 cups flour) in a 9" x 13" casserole dish. If making focaccia, sprinkle on toppings, cover and bake. If making pizza, cover and pre-bake crust without the toppings until lightly browned. Spread toppings, cover and bake until toppings are cooked and cheese is melted, 30 minutes–1 hour, depending on whether the toppings are precooked or raw.

Pancakes

Pour 4–6 individual pancakes on an uncovered, greased baking sheet or make one big pancake in a 9" pie pan or graniteware roaster. Cover and bake 30 minutes for smaller pancakes or 1 hour for a single large pancake.

Tortillas, flatbread, and crêpes

Preheat a cast iron skillet or tortilla griddle. Lightly grease and bake one flatbread at a time, covered with an overturned black roaster. Cook first side for about 5 minutes. No brown spots will appear. Flip over bread and cook another 5 minutes. Don't overcook or you'll get crackers. If you have a parabolic reflector, bake flatbread as if you were using a stovetop skillet.

Solar crackers

Make crackers when the humidity is low. Arrange crackers so they don't touch each other on a lightly greased baking sheet. Bake uncovered or loosely covered with a second overturned tray. Vent the cooker door (1/16 inch is enough) to allow excess moisture to escape. Bake one hour or until lightly browned.

Masonic suns.

Pita chips, croutons and bruschetta

Slice fresh pita bread into 6–8 wedges, loaves into ¾-inch cubes or baguettes into thin slices. Drizzle bread with oil or use a pastry brush and toss or sprinkle with salt and dried herbs. Arrange in a single layer on the baking tray and bake uncovered or loosely covered until lightly brown and crispy, 1½–2 hours or more depending on the temperature.

17
Hearth bread

"Building and baking in a wood-fired earthen oven restores the simplicity of bread by returning you to essentials: earth, water, air, and fire."
— Kiko Denzer, *Build Your Own Earth Oven*

The basics: Those of us who are aficionados of artisan bread agree that no other bread compares to artisan loaves baked directly on the hearth of a wood-fired earth or masonry oven. Heat radiates from all sides of the oven, producing extraordinary oven spring and a thick, crunchy crust. For people who want a super-efficient wood-fired alternative, there is the rocket bread oven.

Baking with fire

The earliest breads were baked in the ashes of a hearth fire or cooked on flat stones heated by fire. Enclosed hearth ovens improved the efficiency of cooking by trapping the heat inside a small space.

An earth oven is a simple, beehive-shaped design built of cob, a mixture of earth, sand, clay and straw. Variations on the earth oven are still in use all over the world today, such as the Spanish *horno* (OHR-noh) brought to the American Southwest in the 1500s along with European wheat bread. The most basic earth ovens have one chamber. A small, hot-burning fire heats up the clay and sand (earth acts as a thermal mass to store heat). An outer straw insulation layer retains the heat. The fire is allowed to burn down and the ashes are raked out before the bread or other foods are baked.

A door seals the entrance during baking. The oven cools down gradually over several hours (large ovens retain heat for as long as 24 hours). Two-chamber designs separate the lower wood-burning chamber from the upper chamber in which food is placed so that the fire can burn continuously while food is baking.

The central advantage of earth ovens is that they can be made for little or no money from locally available materials. In addition, earth ovens can burn scrap wood, small diameter trees from forest thinning projects, or other biomass materials, making good use of cast-off resources.

Energy efficiency and community ovens

The main drawback to baking in your own backyard earth oven is that an earth oven is not energy efficient for small volumes of food. The solution is to build a communal oven and bake with your neighbors.

Before the Industrial Revolution, European villages had a village oven presided over by the village baker. Because fuelwood was scarce for much of European history, firing would only happen once a week. Housewives would bring their dough to the oven on baking day. Each baker would slash the top of her bread with a distinctive branding pattern so she could retrieve it after baking. Distinctive bread stamps were also popular.

Today, the growing popularity of cob earth ovens is reviving the idea of the neighborhood bread oven. Community gardens, community centers, community kitchens, schools, hospitals, and public parks are all great places to build an earth oven for public use. An earth oven workshop is a fun neighborhood project for all ages.

It also makes ecological sense to use the heat of a cooling oven for a variety of projects, from baking other foods to drying fruits and vegetables, incubating sourdough or yogurt cultures and even drying clothing. "Wherever there is a tradition of baking bread in a wood-fired oven, there is also a host of other traditional foods, from slow-cooked casseroles to baked vegetables, that make use of the oven's waning heat," say Jeffrey Alford and Naomi Duguid in *Flatbreads & Flavors*.

The best book available on the construction and use of cob earth ovens is Kiko Denzer's Build Your Own Earth Oven. *If you are interested in brick or stone masonry ovens, see* The Bread Builders *by Daniel Wing and Alan Scott.*

Earth ovens can even be designed to be mobile, so they can be carried around to fairs and other events (see illustration on next page).

[**"Lord" comes from the Anglo-Saxon word hlaford, "loaf ward," the person who presides over the communal oven**]

Byzantine limestone bread stamp, 10–11th century. Stamping was usually done on the underside of a loaf.

Baking bread in an earth oven

Baking occurs by a combination of radiation from the oven walls, conduction from the oven floor directly into the loaf and convection of hot air swirling around the oven chamber. There are several skills required to successfully bake in an earth oven:

❖ The biggest skill needed to use an earth oven is learning how to build a proper fire — small but hot. The fire is started near the door of the oven. The logs or bundles of twigs or straw must be stacked so as to allow good air circulation through the fire. The fire is then pushed against the back wall of the oven and more wood is added. If you have made a proper fire, the flames will arch across the top of the oven chamber and leap out the front like tongues of fire from the mouth of a medieval dragon. The fire is allowed to burn at least an hour and sometimes several hours, depending on the size of the oven, until the entire mass of the oven is heated through. In a one-chamber oven, the fire is allowed to burn down, the ashes are raked out and then the door is set into the opening to allow the heat to equalize for a bit to prevent hot spots from scorching the dough.

❖ You will learn to judge how long your oven must be heated before it can be used for baking. Use an oven thermometer or develop your intuition by sticking your hand and arm into the oven chamber to judge how hot it is. A fully heated earth oven will reach 600–700°F/316–371°C, perfect for four-minute pizzas and flatbreads. As the oven cools down, it becomes suitable for artisan loaves, pan breads, and other baked or roasted foods.

❖ Another skill is learning to match the oven heating time with the bread dough proofing time so that both the oven and the dough are ready at the same time.

Baking tips

❖ Loaves and flatbreads are transferred into the oven using a peel dusted with semolina.

❖ Earth ovens retain steam very well, producing excellent oven spring and artisan-style bread crusts. As in a conventional oven, many people place a small cast iron frying pan near the door for producing extra steam.

❖ The hot coals raked out of an earth oven can be used in a barbeque grill.

Super energy-efficient bread baking

If you want a very energy efficient, wood-burning oven for baking bread, consider a rocket bread oven, a modification of the rocket stove, a one-burner stove made from inexpensive materials like used tin cans and old sections of stovepipe. The stove was invented by Dr. Larry Winiarski, a researcher with the Aprovecho Research Institute, a non-profit research and education center that promotes appropriate technology, sustainable forestry, organic agriculture and permaculture. Thick insulation around the combustion chamber and chimney keeps the fire above 1,100°F/593°C for nearly complete combustion. The rocket bread oven funnels the heat up through an insulated 55-gallon drum for energy efficient convection baking. Rocket stoves and ovens can burn tree branches, twigs, wood scraps, or most any small biomass materials. Aprovecho's booklets, *Capturing Heat I & II* provide instructions for building a rocket stove and bread/pizza oven (appendix C).

Street bakers.

18
Old bread

"Give me yesterday's Bread, this Day's Flesh, and last Year's Cyder."
— Benjamin Franklin, *Poor Richard's Almanac*

The basics: Back in the days when bread baking was a communal affair, a large loaf of peasant bread or a stack of pitas might have had to last for a week or two … or longer. Stale bread was a fact of life. Use leftover or freshly-prepared sourdough bread as the base for a variety of delicious dishes.

What to do with leftover, dried or stale breads

❖ Use dry cubes (croutons) of bread or torn pieces of pita bread or sourdough tortillas in salad, stuffing, bread pudding, Italian strata casseroles and French toast.

❖ In medieval Europe, peasants lived on sop, a piece of stale bread soaked in broth. Today, French onion soup is still topped with a slice of bread.

❖ In Spanish and Mexican cooking, stale tortillas are used to make tortilla soup.

❖ More-than-toast: Italian bruschetta is just thinly sliced toast with flavorful toppings and served as an appetizer. Garlic bread is another variation.

❖ Brush pita wedges with a little oil, salt and herbs or spices and lightly toast to make pita chips for dipping.

❖ Recycle bread crumbs back into your next batch of bread dough for extra texture.

❖ There's always feeding the birds or the compost pile.

❧ Croutons ❧

I make extra loaves of pan bread for making croutons. Slice the cooled bread into ¾" cubes and spread out to dry on a large cookie tray. Because I live in arid Arizona, I just set out the tray to air dry over a couple of days. In humid climates, dry the cubes in an electric food dryer or bake the croutons at 350°F/177°C until dry but not browned. To make herbed croutons, toss bread cubes with a little olive oil and dried herbs (try oregano, savory, rosemary and thyme). Spread croutons on a greased baking sheet and toast 5–10 minutes, or until browned.

❧ Bread crumbs ❧

Grind plain croutons into crumbs in a food processor or blender. I store bread crumbs in the freezer to have them on hand whenever necessary. Sauté fresh (moist) bread crumbs in a little olive oil or melted Earth Balance™ with minced garlic or garlic powder to make a tasty topping for casseroles and steamed vegetables.

❧ Bread salad ❧

In Tuscany, bread salad is known as *panzanella*. In Arabic countries, torn flatbread is used to make *fattoush*. Use bread that is partially dried, or lightly toast and cool before using. Add seasonal vegetables, greens and herbs and toss with your favorite dressing. The bread soaks up the dressing and vegetable juices.

❧ Coconut French toast ❧

Another classic vegan French toast recipe is made with a combination of blended banana and milk. Bananas make an excellent egg substitute. Add a few strawberries or blueberries to either purée for a fruity flavor.

This recipe is a modification of the "Fronch" toast in Veganomicon, *by Isa Chandra Moskowitz and Terry Romero. The coconut milk substitutes for soy creamer to create a subtle tropical flavor. The garbanzo flour thickens the dipping mixture and adds a savory, "eggy" flavor.*

4–6 thick slices of bread
½ cup regular or lite coconut milk
½ cup non-dairy milk (plain or vanilla)
2 tablespoons cornstarch
¼ cup fine garbanzo flour
Canola oil or melted Earth Balance™ for frying

1. Dry bread slices overnight. Alternatively, the bread can be dried until crisp and stored until needed.
2. In a 2-quart bowl, whisk together milks and flours.
3. Dip both sides of each slice of bread in liquid and fry each side about 2 minutes, or until golden brown.

❧ Bread pudding ❧

Use the French toast recipe above to make bread pudding. Substitute dry croutons. Add sweetener to taste. Bake pudding in a greased, uncovered casserole dish for 20 minutes at 350°F/177°C or until lightly browned.

❧ Colorful holiday stuffing ❧

If you prefer crusty stuffing, bake it in a shallow baking dish and allow it to brown on top. When not using homemade vegetable stock, I like Image Foods No Chicken Broth™.

1 medium loaf of sourdough bread baked in a pan (about 1 lb)
½ cup Earth Balance™
1 cup chopped yellow onion
1 cup sliced celery
1 cup grated carrots
1 cup chopped Granny Smith apple or other tart apple variety
1 cup dried cranberries
¾ cup chopped pecans
Soy sauce or tamari to taste
Vegetable broth as needed

1. Turn the bread into ¾" cubed croutons. Dry until crisp.
2. Preheat oven to 375°F/191°C.
3. In a medium pot, melt Earth Balance™ over medium-high heat and sauté onion, celery and carrot until onions are translucent. Set aside.
4. In a large bowl, toss croutons with apple, cranberries and pecans. Stir in sauté mixture. Sprinkle soy sauce to taste, then mix in enough vegetable broth to moisten (don't make it too soggy).
5. Spread mixture in a large, buttered casserole dish about 2 inches deep. Or do what I do because I don't have a large enough casserole—use a stainless steel mixing bowl. Cover with casserole lid or foil and bake 20 minutes to heat through.
6. Remove cover and bake another 20 minutes uncovered. If you like a browned surface, broil for a few minutes before serving.

For a vegetarian treat, stuff a large winter squash with this savory, fruity stuffing before baking.

❧ Any-fruit brown Betty ❧

A brown Betty is an old-fashioned American dessert made of layers of sweetened fruit and buttered bread crumbs. Use fewer bread crumbs and sugar if desired.

4 cups thinly sliced apples or other fresh or canned fruit (peel if desired)
1 teaspoon lemon juice
¾ cup dry bread crumbs
¾ cup brown sugar or date sugar
Cinnamon to taste
2 teaspoons Earth Balance™ or canola oil

1. Preheat oven to 350°F/177°C. Toss fruit with lemon juice to prevent browning.
2. In separate bowl, mix bread crumbs, sugar and cinnamon.
3. Grease an 8" x 8" round or square baking dish.
4. Alternate layers of fruit and the bread-sugar mixture, ending with a layer of crumbs. Sprinkle more cinnamon on top if desired. Dot top with Earth Balance™ or drizzle with canola oil.
5. Cover and bake 30 minutes. Uncover and bake until fruit is softened and top is lightly browned.

Part V
Appendix

"In American English, the words 'bread' and 'dough' are slang for money. A 'bread winner' is a person who earns money to keep their family going and a 'bread basket' often refers to a geographical region that has a principle grain supply."

— Jan Scholl, "Breads and Other Cultures,
Penn State College of Agricultural Sciences Cooperative Extension

A
Mail order sourdough cultures

"Let there be work, bread, water and salt for all."
— Nelson Mandela

Breadtopia.com

www.breadtopia.com. This bread-baking supply company is run by a couple in Fairfield, Iowa. They sell fresh and dried versions of a wheat starter. The website also includes free online bread making videos.

Friends of Carl

www.carlsfriends.org. Carl Griffith was a sourdough enthusiast who died in 2000 at the age of 80. His 1847 Oregon Trail Sourdough Starter is still available from his friends (dried ½ oz packets) for the cost of a self-addressed stamped envelope.

GEM Cultures

www.gemcultures.com. GEM Cultures is a small, family-owned business that sells fermentation starters for bread, dairy, soy, and kombucha. If you are a fan of fermented foods, you'll want to check out their offerings. The company offers four sourdough cultures. Two are wheat-based (Cultured Crêpes Leaven and Cool Rise Natural Leaven) and a third is 100% rye. They also sell a gluten-free culture maintained in brown rice flour — the only gluten-free sourdough culture available commercially; this culture can also be fed with other gluten-free flours of your choice. GEM sourdough cultures are shipped live.

GEM Cultures sells the only 100% rye and gluten-free sourdough cultures.

The Baker's Catalogue (King Arthur Flour)

www.kingarthurflour.com. King Arthur Flour is an employee-owned business that first began in 1790. The Baker's Catalogue sells a huge range of baking ingredients and supplies such as high quality flours, including Sir Lancelot Hi-Gluten Flour, bakeware and utensils. Their Classic Fresh Sourdough Starter is "descended from ancestors that have been bubbling away ... in New England for over 250 years." The culture is shipped live. Avoid the one-time-use fake "sourdough" powders.

I have some of King Arthur Flour's Classic Fresh Sourdough Starter culture. It is a medium riser and has an excellent, medium-sour flavor.

Sourdoughs International

www.sourdo.com. Sourdoughs International is the project of Dr. Ed Wood, a retired pathologist and doctor who spent much of his working life in Saudi Arabia. He has collected and studied sourdough cultures as a hobby for more than 50 years. Wood has collected dozens of authentic, traditional sourdough cultures from around the world. Each culture has a distinctive flavor, texture and leavening time. Wood is also the author of *Classic Sourdoughs* (appendix C), which provides detailed information for his cultures.

The cultures come dehydrated and so require special pampering (extra warmth and moisture) to activate them. The company suggests making a proofing box out of a Styrofoam cooler and a 25-watt incandescent bulb connected to a dimmer switch. It is possible to use your oven on a low setting no greater than 90°F/32°C, too. Complete activation directions are provided with each order and can also be found in *Classic Sourdoughs*.

Sourdoughs International makes the guarantee that if directions in Classic Sourdoughs *are followed correctly and a culture fails to "start," it will be replaced within one month of shipping.*

Here are the company's own descriptions for each culture:

Australia (Tasmanian Devil)

"Produces breads with a distinctive flavor and texture. It has the added versatility of being ideal for spelt and kamut flours."

Austria

"This starter is from the old section of Innsbruck. The culture is especially adapted to rye flours, rises somewhat slowly and produces one of the more sour doughs."

The Giza culture "could be the progeny of the one that made man's first bread and is similar to the one we used to recreate that first bread in Egypt for the National Geographic."

Bahrain

"It rises well and is one of the most sour."

Egypt: The Giza culture

"The bakery where this sourdough was found dated straight back to antiquity and was literally in the shadow of the pyramids. The dough rises well and is moderately sour."

Egypt: The Red Sea culture

"From one of the oldest ethnic bakeries in Egypt. It was found in Hurghada on the shore of the Red Sea when it was still just a village. The bread was actually placed on the village street to rise. It has a mild flavor and works well in bread machines."

Finland

"Hard to describe, as the wonderful and distinctive flavor and aroma it imparts are truly 'indescribable.' It rises well."

France

"From a small bakery on the outskirts of Paris that has been in business for over 150 years. The starter rises very well and the dough has one of the mildest sourdough flavors."

Italian Cultures (includes two)

"Both from the Naples area, where the first pizza was made in the 1800s ... among the best we have ever used, consistently producing fabulous breads that are flavorful and that can be quite sour."

Authentic San Francisco sourdough.

New Zealand: (includes two)

"One of the easiest and best choices for the novice sourdough baker. It is a lovely sourdough that works for everything from whole wheat, potato, sweet breads etc."

Original San Francisco

"Authentic San Francisco sourdough," *L. sanfranciscensis.*

Russia

"From the village of Palekh two hundred miles northeast of Moscow. A fast leavening culture, handles heavy Russian whole wheat doughs very well and appears ideal for automatic home bread machines."

Saudi Arabia

"Rises moderately well and has one of the most distinctive flavors of all the cultures."

South Africa

"The only sourdough culture we are aware of that leavens whole-wheat better than it does white flour. The flavor is truly unique, and when combined with 100% whole wheat, the texture, sourness and flavor are unsurpassed. The nutty flavor persists and white sourdough breads made with this culture are quite different from those prepared with our other sourdough cultures."

Yukon

Obtained from a Yukon prospector. "Wonderful flavor."

Sample leavening times for Sourdoughs International cultures

As you can see, cultures greatly vary in their speed of leavening. The first column is the time it takes to reach peak leavening time after being removed from the refrigerator. The middle column is the time a culture stays at peak leavening power before going dormant. The third column is the time it takes for a loaf of bread to double in volume during proofing.

	Activation time	Peak leavening time	Proofing time
Austria	9 hours	6 hours	3 hours
Bahrain	9–11 hours	6–7 hours	3 hours
France	6–8 hours	4–5 hours	2–3 hours
Giza	9 hours	6 hours	3 hours
Red Sea	1½–2 hours	2–3 hours	1½–2 hours
Russia	1–1½ hours	2–3 hours	1–2 hours
San Francisco	6–8 hours	4–5 hours	2–3 hours
Saudi Arabia	9 hours	6 hours	3 hours
Yukon	6 hours	4 hours	2–3 hours

B
Sourdough & bread troubleshooting

"I am very particular about the way that I like my bread, which may seem a little peculiar, but we all have our little eccentricities don't we!"

— Sylvester Graham

Problems with your sourdough culture

Help! I've killed my culture!

❖ Next time, dry and freeze some culture as an emergency backup.

❖ Feed, water and aerate your starter on a weekly basis even if you do not bake. Give the extra starter to friends. Someday they may return the favor.

How to make your bread milder in flavor

❖ Get a naturally mild, fast-rising culture, such as Sourdoughs International's Russia or Red Sea cultures (appendix A).

❖ Sweeten or wash your culture as described in chapter 3 to dilute the acids and rebalance the microbe populations.

❖ Start over and use the "pineapple juice solution" in chapter 3 to reduce the growth of *Leuconostoc* bacteria.

❖ Do a fast proof in a warm location to give the bacteria less time to multiply. Avoid temperatures over 80°F/27°C which encourage the growth of unwanted types of bacteria.

How to make your bread more sour-flavored:

❖ If you have a very fast starter and use it very frequently (several times a week or more), the bacteria may not have enough time to reproduce. Keep a couple of jars and rotate them.

❖ Get a more naturally sour, slow-rising culture, such as a San Francisco starter containing *L. sanfranciscensis* (appendix A).

❖ Proof the bread in a cool environment, such as the refrigerator, for a slow rise that allows lots of time for the lactobacteria to produce acid.

❖ Extend proofing time by degassing, reshaping and reproofing.

Problems with bread baking

The dough will not rise

❖ The yeast is present in insufficient amounts. Give the culture a longer activation time.

❖ The yeast may have died. Start over with a new culture.

❖ The water or proofing temperature was too hot, killing the yeast.

❖ The water or proofing temperature is too cool. Give the yeast more warmth.

❖ The dough is too dry and stiff. Use a wetter dough.

❖ The dough contains too much sugar or fat for the yeast to lift.

❖ The dough contains too much salt.

The bread did not have sufficient oven spring

❖ The dough was underproofed.

❖ The dough was not sprayed with water or oiled before baking, causing the crust to harden prematurely. This is especially a problem in arid climates.

The bread has risen too high

❖ Did you leave out the salt? Salt slows down fermentation.

❖ If the dough has not yet been baked, re-knead and re-proof it.

❖ If you bake over-proofed bread, it will fall during baking due to lack of structural support.

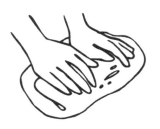

The crust did not brown enough

❖ If making artisan bread, use a higher baking temperature or move the oven rack closer to the top of the oven to receive more radiating heat.

❖ If making loaf bread, the pan may be too bright, reflecting away heat; use a darker pan.

The crust is too dark

❖ The oven temperature was too high.

❖ Glazes can cause excessive darkening.

The crust has excessive or unsightly cracking

❖ The dough was not mixed or kneaded properly, resulting in insufficient gluten development.

❖ The dough was too dry.

❖ The dough was underproofed, causing excessive oven spring.

❖ Slash loaves before baking to control the oven spring.

The crust is too thick

❖ The dough was too dry.

❖ The dough was not proofed long enough.

❖ The loaf was baked too long at an insufficiently high temperature.

The crumb is dense or gummy

❖ The dough was too dry.

❖ The dough was too wet.

❖ The percentage of gluten-free flours was too high.

❖ The dough was not kneaded long enough.

❖ The dough was not proofed long enough.

❖ The dough was overproofed and collapsed in the oven.

❖ Runaway enzyme reactions broke too many starch molecules into sugar (chapter 7).

❖ The bread was not baked long enough.

❖ Cool loaves on a wire rack to prevent the bottom crust from becoming soggy.

The bread contains one or more large holes

❖ The dough was not mixed or kneaded properly, resulting in insufficient gluten development.

❖ The air was not pressed out of the dough during shaping. This is especially a problem with dough that is rolled out, spread with a filling, and rolled into a spiral loaf.

❖ The dough was underproofed, causing excessive oven spring.

❖ The dough was overproofed.

Engraving of a miller grinding flour.

C
Resources

*"Bread and water — these are the things nature requires.
For such things no man is too poor, and whosoever can limit his desire
to them alone can rival Jupiter for happiness."*
— Seneca

Organic grains & flours

Some of these companies sell their complete line of products directly to consumers; others sell primarily through natural foods cooperatives, buying clubs and retail stores.

Anson Mills, www.ansonmills.com
Arrowhead Mills, www.arrowheadmills.com
Bluebird Grain Farms, www.bluebirdgrainfarms.com
Bob's Red Mill, www.bobsredmill.com
Coop Directory Service, www.coopdirectory.org.
Eden Organic, www.edenfoods.com
Giusto's Vita Grain, www.giustos.com
Heartland Mill, www.heartlandmill.com
Kamut® Association, www.kamut.com
Montana Flour & Grains, www.montanaflour.com
The Baker's Catalogue, www.kingarthurflour.com
United Natural Foods, www.unitedbuyingclubs.com.
Vita-Spelt, www.purityfoods.com.

Grain milling

Country Living Grain Mills, www.countrylivinggrainmills.com. Highly-rated mid-priced brand. Hand and electric models.

Flour Power: A Guide To Modern Home Grain Milling, Marleeta F. Basey. 2004, Jermar Press, 288 pages. Everything you need to know about choosing and using a hand- or electric-powered grain mill and much more.

The Human Powered Home: Choosing Muscles Over Motors, Tamara Dean. 2008, New Society Publishers, 272 pages. A detailed instruction manual on constructing treadle- and pedal-powered machines, including plans for converting a hand-cranked grain mill and an electric blender to bicycle power.

Hand-cranked Country Living Grain Mill™.

Lehman's, www.lehmans.com. Originally servicing Amish people, Lehman's has expanded to provide a multitude of products for "people world-wide who choose to live with little or no reliance on electricity, or who think that the old ways are better than the new ways." Sells their own low-priced, well-rated grain mill (the one I use) plus other highly-rated brands like Country Living™ and Diamant™.

Bread books, DVDs & Web sites

Ancient Egypt Research Associates, www.aeraweb.org/ lost_city_bakeries.asp. Read about the archeological excavation of an ancient Egyptian bakery and Dr. Ed Wood's recreation of ancient Egyptian sourdough bread baking.

Artisan Baking Across America, Maggie Glezer. 2000, Artisan, 256 pages. This book provides a good exposure to some of the leading artisan bakeries in the U.S. The pages are thick and sturdy — a plus for any cookbook — and the pictures and instructions for each recipe are beautiful and thorough.

Artisan Breads DVD, King Arthur Flour Company. Step-by-step instruction on mixing, shaping, proofing and baking high-hydration artisan dough with a sourdough-like poolish from master baker Michael Jubinsky. 50 minutes. Other DVDs in the series include Sweet Dough and Baking With Kids.

The Bread Builders: Hearth Loaves and Masonry Ovens, Daniel Wing and Alan Scott. 1999, Chelsea Green, 250 pages. One of the best books available on sourdough fermentation, artisan bread baking and wheat and rye flours. The second half of the book is about the construction and use of brick masonry ovens.

Bread Science: the Chemistry and Craft of Making Bread, Emily Buehler. Two Blue Books, 2006, www.twobluebooks.com. Buehler is a professional baker and has a doctorate in chemistry. Very detailed book on the chemistry and microbiology of preferments and sourdough cultures, fermentation and baking.

Build Your Own Earth Oven: A Low-Cost, Wood-Fired Mud Oven; Simple Sourdough Bread; Perfect Loaves, Kiko Denzer. 2000, Hand Print Press, 132 pages. Cob ovens and sourdough.

Capturing Heat I & II, Aprovecho Research Center, www.aprovecho.net. Instructions for building a rocket bread oven, a solar box cooker and a solar parabolic reflector.

Classic Sourdoughs: A Home Baker's Handbook, Ed Wood. 2002, Ten Speed Press, 224 pages. One of the few books that deals exclusively with real sourdough baking that doesn't include baker's yeast. It also includes information on using sourdough cultures with bread machines.

Flatbreads & Flavors: A Baker's Atlas, Jeffrey Alford and Naomi Duguid. 1995, William Morrow Cookbooks, 464 pages. Two decades of travel through Asia, Europe, the Mediterranean, North Africa, and North America. A travelogue and cookbook.

Guns, Germs and Steel: The Fates of Human Societies, Jared Diamond. 1999, W. W. Norton & Company, 480 pages. How geography led to the advent and spread of wheat-based agriculture in the Middle East (among many other topics).

Wood's out-of-print book World Sourdoughs From Antiquity *traces the history of sourdough baking from ancient Egypt to modern times. It includes an account of Wood's National Geographic Society-funded experiments catching wild sourdough cultures in Egypt and baking ancient Egyptian emmer bread.*

Handbook of Dough Fermentations, Karel Kulp (Editor), Klaus Lorenz (Editor). 2003, CRC Press, 328 pages. History from ancient times to the present. Microbiology of yeast and lactobacilli fermentations.

The Laurel's Kitchen Bread Book, Laurel Robertson, Carol Flinders, Bronwen Godfrey. 2003, Random House Trade Paperbacks, 464 pages. Most of the recipes are not sourdough. however, it provides instructions for making Flemish desem.

Local Breads, Daniel Leader and Lauren Chattman. 2007, W. W. Norton, 448 pages. In this book, Leader compiles a strong portfolio of Europe's best artisan bakeries. He spent several years visiting and working with leading bakers throughout Europe, and his insights are nicely conveyed in this book.

Renaissance kitchen.

The Magic of Fire: Hearth Cooking: One Hundred Recipes for the Fireplace or Campfire, William Rubel. 2002, Ten Speed Press, 296 pages. Open fire hearth baking.

Peter Reinhart's Whole Grain Breads: New Techniques, Extraordinary Flavor, Peter Reinhart. 2007, Ten Speed Press, 309 pages. Reinhart is master artisan bread baker with decades of experience. This is his most recent book. Check out his many previous books, too, such as *The Bread Baker's Apprentice*.

The Sunny Side of Cooking: Solar cooking and other ecologically friendly cooking methods for the 21st century, Lisa Rayner. 2007, Lifeweaver LLC, 128 pages, www.lisarayner.com. Vegan cookbook on how to choose and use solar cookers.

Wild Fermentation: The Flavor, Nutrition, and Craft of Live-Culture Foods, Sandor Ellix Katz. 2003, Chelsea Green Publishing Company, 200 pages. Fun-to-read book on the "culture" and history of fermented plant foods.

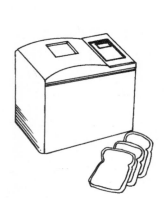

Worldwide sourdoughs from your bread machine, Donna German, Ed Wood. 1994, Bristol Publishing, 176 pages. How to use Sourdoughs International's cultures in a bread machine.

Books & seed sources for growing wheat

Bountiful Gardens, www.bountifulgardens.org. Untreated open-pollinated heirloom seeds. Rare and unusual varieties.

The Bread Book, Thom Leonard. 1990, East West Health Books. Unlike many bread books, this book delves into the steps required to grow and care for one's own wheat patch. Leonard is an advocate of becoming even more intimate with the bread one bakes (being a participant in every step of its production, from seed to bread), and his message is both passionate and convincing.

Cornucopia II: A Source Book of Edible Plants, Stephen Facciola. 2nd ed. 1998, Kampong Publications, 713 pages. Comprehensive reference book. Dozens of varieties of grains described.

The Land Institute, www.landinstitute.org. Salina, KS. The Land Institute researches perennial versions of annual grains, including wheat and rye, which will function like natural prairie ecosystems.

One Straw Revolution, Masanobu Fukuoka. Rodale Press, 1978 and **The Natural Way of Farming**, Japan Publications, 1985. Free online at www.soilandhealth.org/01aglibrary/01aglibwel-come.html. Fukuoka (1914–2008) was a Japanese farmer/philosopher. His "natural farming" involves no plowing, machinery, fossil fuels, artificial fertilizers or pesticides, no prepared compost, and little weeding.

Seed Savers Exchange, www.seedsavers.org. Non-profit organization that facilitates the exchange of heirloom seeds between gardeners and farmers.

Small-Scale Grain Raising: An Organic Guide to Growing, Processing, and Using Nutritious Whole Grains for Home Gardeners and Local Farmers, Gene Logsdon. 2009, Chelsea Green, 320 pages. New edition of the 1977 classic. It includes specifics on growing corn, wheat, oats, rye, barley, buckwheat, millet, rice, and more. Includes information on planting, diseases and pests, harvesting, storing and processing grains.

Cob oven workshop providers

Barefoot Builder, www.barefootbuilder.com.
Cob Cottage Company, www.cobcottage.com.
Kiko Denzer, www.intabas.com/kikodenzer.html.
Seven Generations Natural Builders, http://sgnb.com/intro.php.

Index

G

Acknowledgements

Zackery Zdinack for the drawings of solar cookers. Life Drawing & Education, P.O. Box 1314, Flagstaff, AZ 86002, www.lifedraw.com, wildlife@lifedraw.com.

For proofreading and book suggestions: Leah Berger, Brenda Broussard, Dan Frazier, Kate Mareck, Carleton Sheppard, and Ben Williams.

Special thanks to Leah Berger for writing an off-the-cuff essay that turned into the preface.

Sandor Ellix Katz, author of *Wild Fermentation: The Flavor, Nutrition, and Craft of Live-Culture Foods*. His book was my source of inspiration for the title of *Wild Bread*.

My husband, Dan Frazier, for eating and critiquing my bread and keeping my kitchen clean.

My cats Pablo and Sasha for keeping me company while I wrote this book.

About the author

The daughter of a chemist and a biologist, Lisa Rayner has long had an interest in the natural world. She spent much of her time exploring the forest around her Delaware home.

Lisa hated cooking growing up. Then, in 1985 she became vegetarian, and soon after, vegan. She spent the next year-and-a-half teaching herself to cook and in the process discovered she enjoyed it. In 1996 Lisa obtained a word processor while dumpster-diving and subsequently wrote her first book *Growing Food in the Southwest Mountains*. She published the 3rd edition of the book in 2002. Lisa published a small community newspaper, *Flagstaff Tea Party*, and ran a community currency program called Flagstaff Neighborly Notes from 2000–2002. She published her second book, *The Sunny Side of cooking*, in 2007.

Lisa has a Bachelor of Science degree in Natural Resource Interpretation from Northern Arizona University. She is a graduate of the 1993 Black Mesa Permaculture Project's permaculture design certification course.

Lisa lives with her husband Dan Frazier in Flagstaff, Arizona. She teaches sustainable cooking and permaculture workshops in northern Arizona. In her spare time, Lisa is a progressive political activist. In 2008 she won the Martin-Springer Institute Moral Courage Award and the Friends of Flagstaff's Future Liveable Community Award for her volunteer efforts. She is currently working on several books with bioregional and sustainable themes.

Also available at www.LisaRayner.com

Growing food in the Southwest Mountains: A Permaculture Approach to Home Gardening Above 6,500 Feet in Arizona, New Mexico, Southern Colorado and Southern Utah

By Lisa Rayner
Illustrations by Zackery Zdinak
3rd ed. © 2002
Flagstaff Tea Party
Full color cover
128 pages, perfect bound
ISBN 0-9719565-02

Whether you are a weekend gardener or an avid permaculturalist, this book will help you grow food under the challenging circumstances in the high altitude Southwest: dry weather, high winds, intense sunlight, cold nights, insect pests & much more.

"Lisa Rayner's new edition of this little masterpiece
provides you with principles for living and eating in harmony
with northern Arizona's natural habitats."

— Dr. Gary Paul Nabhan, Author,
Coming Home to Eat: the Pleasures and Politics of Local Foods

"If every region in North America had a handbook like this, we would be seven leagues ahead of where we now are in Permaculture education. The author and publishers are to be commended for creating a first-class resource."

— Cathy Holt, *The Permaculture Activist* magazine

"Lisa Rayner's book is a very useful guide to how to apply ancient, traditional and modern permaculture and gardening techniques to successful production of nutritious and varied regionally-appropriate foods."

— Jan Busco, author of *Native Plants for High Elevation Western Gardens*

The Sunny Side of Cooking: Solar cooking and other ecologically friendly cooking methods for the 21st century

By Lisa Rayner, 1st ed. © 2007, Lifeweaver LLC
Full color cover, 128 pages, comb bound
ISBN 978-0-9800608-0-5

What if there was a year-round method of cooking that was low cost, powered by sunlight, non-polluting, and easy to do even in college dorms, apartment balconies and off-the-grid locations?
There is: solar cooking.

The Sunny Side of Cooking includes information on:
◉ how to choose the right solar cooker for you
◉ how to adapt your favorite recipes
◉ more than 100 vegetarian recipes & tips
◉ how to safely can foods in a solar cooker
◉ how to create a year-round sustainable cooking system with solar cookers, fireless cookers, pressure cookers, biomass stoves and earth ovens

"This new solar cookbook by Lisa Rayner is beautifully detailed and informative. I highly recommend it both for beginners and experienced solar cooks. Her recipes make one's mouth water just reading them! I know you are in for a lot of pleasure as you explore how your solar cooker fits into your household routine and the variety of foods it can bring to perfection."
— Barbara Prosser Kerr, co-inventor of the Kerr-Cole EcoCooker™
Kerr-Cole Sustainable Living Center, Taylor, AZ

"For as long as I have been associated with Barbara she has been on the lookout for persons to carry forward the knowledge she has accrued over the years. Especially she has wished to foster persons to teach folks in their community to solar cook and to apply the allied practices such as fireless cooking and efficient fuel-wood cooking. Bravo for a thorough and easily understood coverage of the essential topics!"
— James Scott, solar engineer
Kerr-Cole Sustainable Living Center, Snowflake, AZ

Order form for Lifeweaver LLC

Book	Price	Quantity	Total
Wild Bread	$16.95		
The Sunny Side of Cooking	$14.95		
Growing Food in the Southwest Mountains	$12.95		
Shipping and handling (per book)	$3.00		
Books are shipped USPS First Class		*Total*	

Send check or money order (U.S. currency only) to:

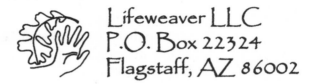

Lifeweaver LLC
P.O. Box 22324
Flagstaff, AZ 86002

Name:_____

Street address or P.O. Box:_____

City: _____ **State:** _____ **Zipcode:** _____

Telephone: _____ (Circle one: home / work / cell)

E-mail: _____

To order online (credit cards accepted)
or for information on wholesale discounts visit
www.LisaRayner.com   Lisa@LisaRayner.com